First published in the United States by
Interweave Press LLC
201 East Fourth Street
Loveland, CO 80537
www.interweave.com

ISBN: 978-1-59668-626-7

Library of Congress Cataloging-in-Publication Data not
available at time of printing.

the crafter's guide to

taking great photos

the best techniques for showcasing your handmade creations

Heidi Adnum

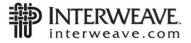

INTERWEAVE.
interweave.com

Contents

Introduction

Even if you're on a budget, this book will help you take great product photographs. All the advice, tips, and tutorials are relevant to crafters and are strictly jargon-free. You'll be guided through the basics of your camera and photography to help you to tell your story. In no time at all, your photographs will be looking great and ready to go. Photography will become more enjoyable and less daunting as your understanding of what makes a photograph successful becomes clearer. Readers of this book will know how important light is for photography and how best to use it to take great product photographs.

When it comes to photography, there's no right or wrong way, but there is better and worse. This book will keep in mind that, most of the time, good product photographs will be:

→ well-lit, using as much natural light as possible;
→ clear, and have at least one part or feature of the product in focus;
→ kept simple, with minimal distractions;
→ able to convey your brand and story at a glance and gain the interest of your customers, answer many of their questions, and help them to remember your product.

Easy-to-follow DIY tutorials for photographic accessories will save you money and make the most out of any lighting situation or setting. Crafters looking for advice and with questions to be answered on their specific product will find that, too. Featured crafters share their stories in the many practitioner spotlights, and the branding, marketing, and merchandising advice will help everyone looking to improve their business as a whole. Along the way, expect to see a treasure trove of hand-picked, excellent product photographs and helpful illustrations.

Whether you're starting from scratch, completely frustrated with your progress to date, or simply looking to improve your technique—this book is for you.

[1] Blueberry Print
Nikon D90
1/80 sec, f/4.8, ISO 800, 48mm
Eve Legris

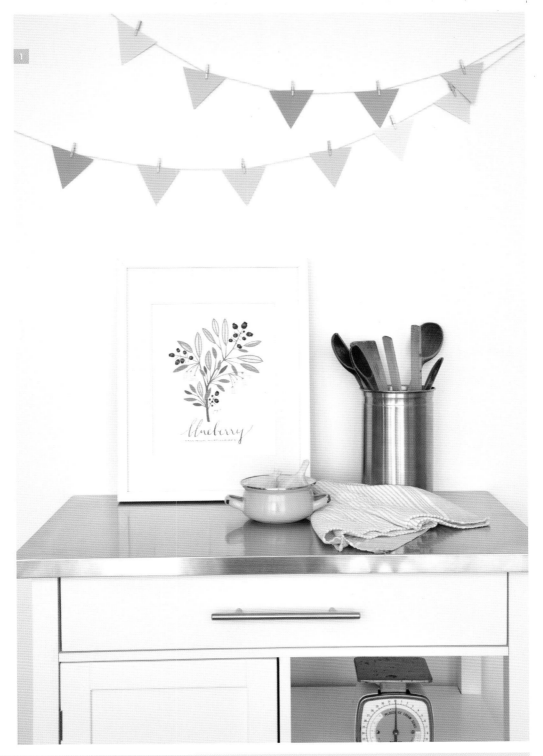

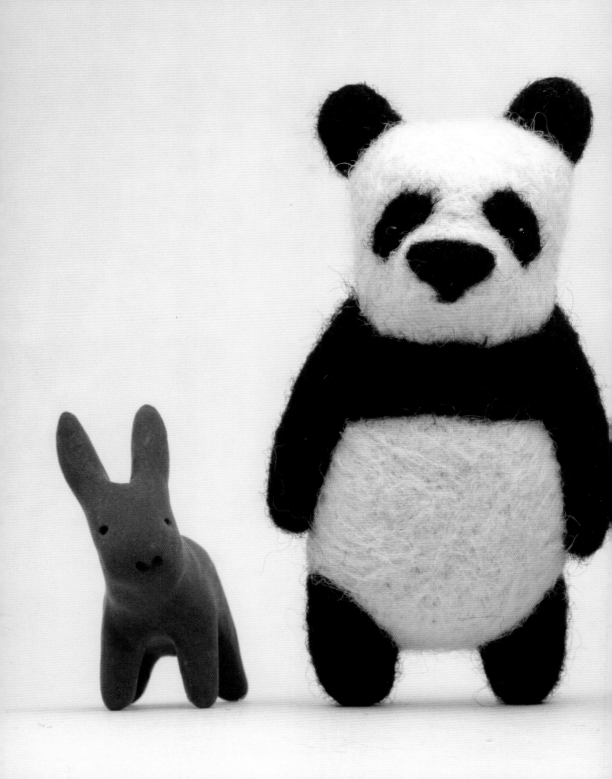

I   GETTING STARTED

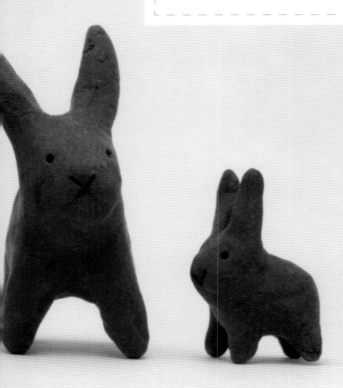

Light

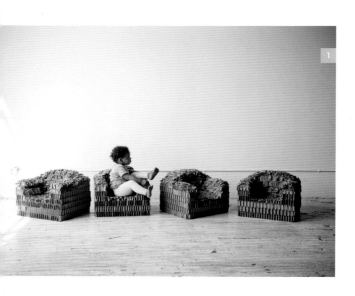

"Photography" means drawing with light: "photo" meaning light and "graph" to write or draw. A photograph is drawn when light enters a camera through a lens and hits a light-sensitive surface, such as film or a digital sensor. The sensor turns the light into readable information, which is then processed (chemically for film or electronically for digital sensors) into an image we can see. So, to better understand photography, we need to understand light.

[1] Rip + Tatter Kid's Chair
Nikon D3X
1/200 sec, f/2.8,
ISO 100, 55mm
Matthew Williams

[2] Teardrop Necklace
Canon EOS 7D
1/1000 sec, f/5.6,
ISO 4000, 135mm
Marie Bee

[3] Blushing in Pink Hand-dyed Dress
Nikon D40
1/200 sec, f/4.6,
ISO 200, 44mm
Galaxie Andrews

[4] Stoneware Vase with Floral Embellishments
Nikon D300
1/125 sec, f/1.4,
ISO 200, 30mm
Christine Tenenholtz

TYPE OF LIGHT

Light is either natural or artificial, soft or hard. Soft light is a source of light that seems big when compared to the object, or has been diffused in some way and creates gentle, pale, and minimal shadows. Hard light is, from the object's point of view, a small directional light source and, as such, creates darker, more distinct shadows. There is no right or wrong light to use for photography in general. But for product photography, you should definitely use softened light, preferably softened natural light, as it will flatter your product and look much nicer than hard light or artificial light.

You can tell almost everything you need to know about a photograph by looking at the shadows. They tell us whether lighting was soft or hard and also give us clues about the size and direction of the light source.

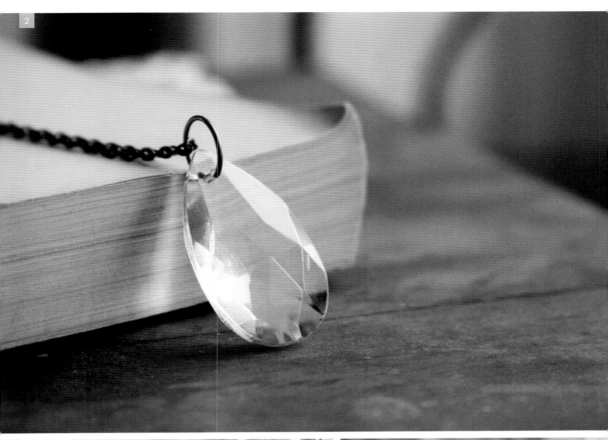

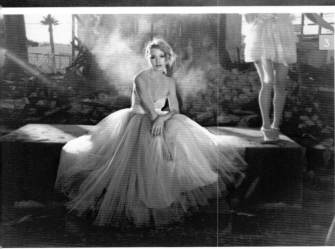

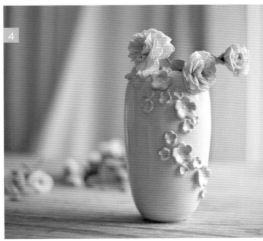

HOW TO USE LIGHT

Backlight

Backlighting (also called "rim lighting") is a popular technique used to separate an object from the background, often creating a warm highlight or a glow around the back or edges of the product. Shadows are created in the foreground.

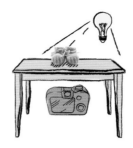

Sidelight

This is a great way to create a gradual lighting effect from one side of the object to the other. The side facing away from the light will be the darkest and will show shadows. Add in a matching light source on the opposite side to create a more balanced effect.

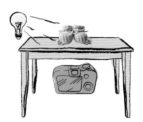

Frontlight

This is a good technique to create a darker looking background. A white background will look a shade of gray if all of the light enters from the front and most of it falls onto the product. Shadows fall behind the product.

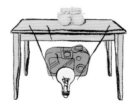

Window light

Window light is the quintessential light for indoor product photography and many other types of photography, too. The window acts as a beautifully large light source. The quality and softness of window light depends on the position and intensity of the sun. That is, sun shining directly through the window is still going to be hard light, so it's best to use window light when the sun isn't shining directly through the window. Window light can be used to create any of the above techniques or, indeed, can be combined with them.

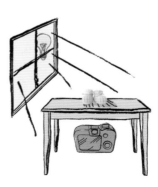

BALANCING LIGHT

Finding the right amount of light for photography is one of the biggest challenges crafters face. Often it is a perceived lack of light in a photograph that is most troublesome. However, there are tips and tricks that will make balancing light much easier.

To increase the amount of light available for your photographs:

→ Go outside. Even on a dull and cloudy day there will be more available light than you think. Cloudy days are ideal for photography, as the clouds act as natural diffusers.

→ Position your product near a large window and shoot there. Windows are perfect as a directional light source, and, depending on the position of your product and the intensity of light, you have a large, soft light that falls on your product from a flattering angle.

→ If you don't have a large window, then a light tent will have a similar effect (see page 54).

→ Reflect more light in to your photograph (see page 58).

→ If the amount of light isn't the problem, but the ever-present rain or wind is, create your own little photographic haven simply by using a bottom-weighted sheet of clear plastic over a clothesline. You can then add in diffusers, which place a barrier between your product and the light. Semi-translucent sheets of plastic, like core flute, or fabric, like muslin, can be taped on the roof/walls. It will be like a clear/white and well-ventilated greenhouse.

→ If you need to use artificial light, invest in cheap household or garden lights, such as desk lamps with adjustable heads—just make sure that their bulbs are white in color and that you diffuse the light. For more on color, see page 22.

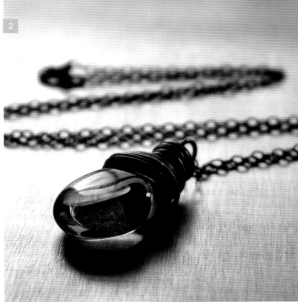

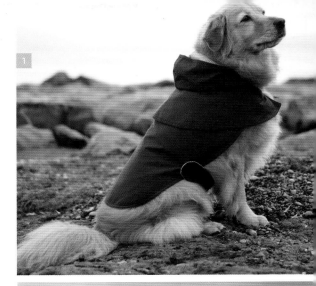

[1] Starboard Anorak
Canon EOS 5D
1/1328 sec, f/2.8, ISO 200, 70mm
Emily Lockhart

[2] Leaf Teardrop Necklace
Nikon Coolpix L100
1/265 sec, f/4.3, ISO 80, 12.2mm
Celia Boaz

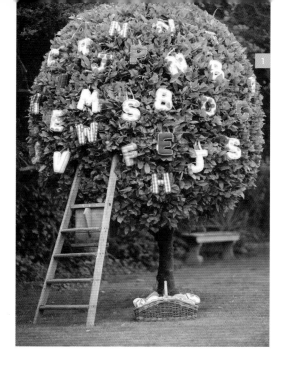

[1] Little Love Letter
Canon EOS 1D MkII
1/320 sec, f/2.0, ISO 50, 100mm
Bill Bradshaw

If your light is usually too strong and your photographs show dark shadows:

→ Diffuse the light. More options include sheer white parchment paper or a white shower curtain. Tape or hang the diffuser over a window or clothesline.

→ Move into the shade—this is naturally diffused light. Remember that clouds are natural light diffusers, so choose to shoot on an overcast day rather than a sunny day.

→ Stay inside and, once again, try window light. Window light can increase the amount of light but it can also diffuse it, especially if you have a sheer, white curtain to pull across.

→ Gradually move the light source further away from your product, or vice versa.

→ Light your product from behind—this lessens the likelihood that strong light is going to overpower the detail and features of your product.

USING FLASH

Flash is the most commonly used artificial light in photography and is built in to almost all digital cameras. Digital cameras use their built-in light meter to quickly measure the amount of light in the scene. On the automatic setting, the flash pops up when your camera has decided that there isn't enough ambient light to make a clear image. Like other undiffused lights, flash is a hard light when used at close range. Due to its size and power, on-camera flash can only cover a fairly small area, so it is often only able to light the object in the foreground. The harsh light creates unnatural glare and can flatten the look of a photograph. On-camera flash can be difficult to work with and, as a general rule, should be avoided for product photography.

The best way to work with flash is to mimic the professionals who, when necessary, use "fill light." Fill light is a small amount of diffused flash added to bring up the foreground of a scene that is otherwise well lit in the background.

FILL LIGHT

On-camera flash

When your image is well exposed in the background but the foreground is a little too dark, you may lose detail in the foreground and it may show dark shadows. Your on-camera flash can be used as a fill light but it may need to be made larger and softer with the aid of a diffuser. This will depend on the size and power of your flash. For the best results, it's often best to ensure that you're using a camera mode other than full automatic.

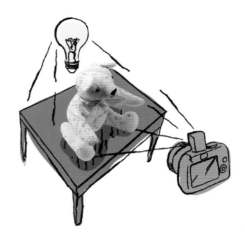

Mode selection

Select a manual or semi-automatic mode (such as macro), so that you have more control over the settings, and turn on the flash.

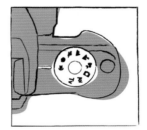

Diffusing on-camera flash

Diffuse or redirect the flash with white paper or card (learn how to make a flash diffuser on page 60) and retake the image. The larger, softer flash will add light to the foreground and won't be so strong that it causes harsh shadows or further loss of detail by "blowing out" the foreground.

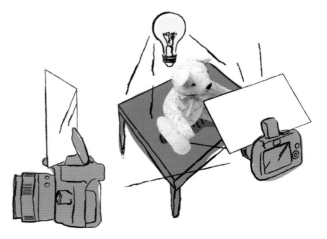

Aperture

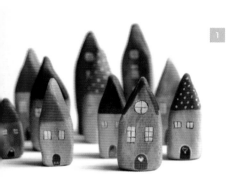

Aperture is how wide the lens opens to allow in light to reach the camera's light-sensitive device, the sensor. Understanding aperture is a photographic concept that can be applied to the human eye: the wider the pupils, the more light is let in, and vice versa. The aperture range on your camera is dependent on your lens.

Aperture is expressed as an f/number (or f/stop) and this is a ratio that represents the amount of light let in by the lens. The smaller the f/number, e.g., f/2, the larger the aperture opening. The larger the f/number, e.g., f/16, the smaller the aperture opening. With every standard increase in f/number, the aperture decreases by half. So, for example, f/2 is a very wide-open lens and large aperture, and will allow in double the amount of light as f/2.8. Conversely, f/2.8, while still a very wide-open lens and large aperture, is a smaller aperture than f/2 and allows in half as much light as f/2.

Quite often there is a relationship between aperture and the "depth of field" of an image. Depth of field (or DoF) is the distance between the nearest and farthest in-focus objects in a photograph.

The larger the aperture, the smaller or more shallow the DoF. Shallow DoF (represented by the smaller f/numbers, e.g., f/1.8–f/4) results in an obvious out-of-focus area in a photograph.

Shallow DoF allows in more light and is a great way to direct attention to your product by blurring the background or surroundings. It removes or softens distractions and can create a dreamy effect.

Large DoF allows in less light and results in more of the photograph being in focus. It is represented by the larger f/numbers (e.g., f/5.6–f/64). Large DoF is the way to show more clearly several products or features at once, even if they are positioned at different points (or depths) in the photograph.

After realizing the importance of light, the next thing you need to know is how a camera actually makes a photograph using the aperture and shutter to create an exposure. Then, color and focus are the next most important elements of product photography.

[1] Little Houses
Canon EOS 50D
1/332 sec, f/4, ISO 1600, 50mm
Rodica Cioplea

[2] Paperphine Fine Natural Paper Yarn
Nikon D200
1/40 sec, f/4, ISO 250, 56mm
Linda Thalmann

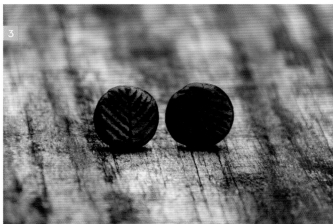

[3] Black Leaves Ear Studs
Canon Digital Rebel XSi
1/125 sec, f/7.1, ISO 200, 250mm
Anastasia Shelyakina

[4] Sand Bow Belt
Canon EOS 5D MkII
1/160 sec, f/2.8, ISO 50, 48mm
Darlingtonia Moccasin Company

[5] Color Pencil Ear Studs
Vivitar ViviCam 3930
1/60 sec, f/3.5, ISO 100, 20mm
Huiyi Tan

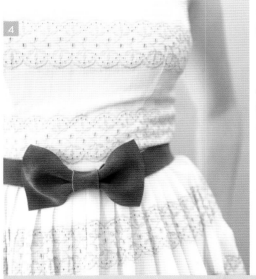

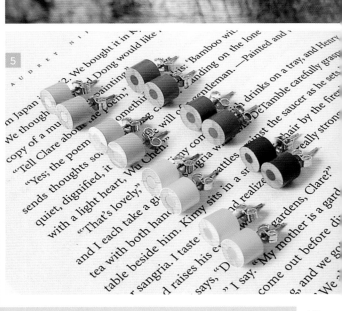

Shutter

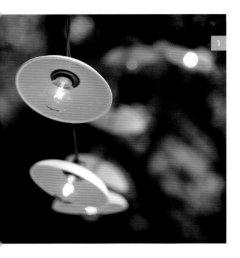

The shutter in your camera is a cover that opens and closes to allow in light to the sensor. The shutter can open very quickly to allow in only a small amount of light, or more slowly to allow in a larger amount of light. Shutter speed is measured and displayed as a fraction of a second and commonly ranges from the slowest speed of several whole seconds to the fastest speeds, which are expressed as thousandths of a second. On your camera's display, the shutter speed may be shown as a fraction, for example 1/100 (one-hundredth of a second) or 1/1 (one whole second), or, it may be displayed as a whole number, e.g., 100 (also one-hundredth of a second) or 1" (also one whole second).

Shutter speed has a close and dependent relationship with aperture: As the aperture opens the lens, the shutter also opens, and combined they allow in light. Normally, the wider open or larger the aperture, the faster the shutter needs to open and close, and vice versa.

On a very bright and sunny day, you need to diffuse the light or seek shade and you might also need to use a fast shutter-speed and small aperture to let in as little light as possible. In low-light conditions or at night, using a large aperture and a slow shutter combines to let in as much light as possible. It's just like opening a door: the wider you open it and the longer you open it for determines how much hot (or cold!) air will get in.

The slower the shutter speed, however, the more likely you are to experience camera shake. Camera shake occurs when the camera moves while the aperture is open. The result is a blurry or a less sharply focused image. Even the most steady-handed person struggles to hold a delicate device like a camera perfectly still. This is why tripods are almost essential for night-time, low-light, or any other low shutter-speed photography.

Shutter speed is very important for the photography of moving objects, as it determines how well-focused they will be in the final image. (Read more about focus on page 24.)

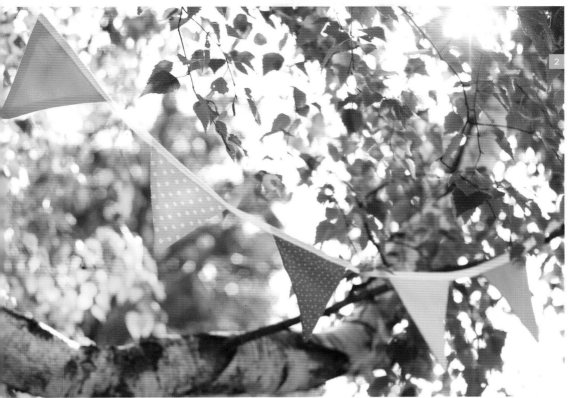

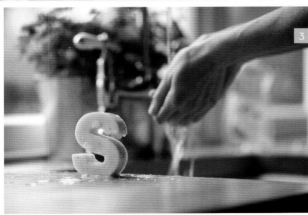

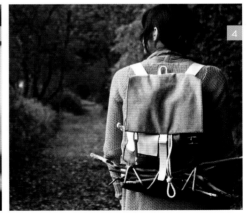

[1] Hand-thrown Disc String Lights
Nikon D3
1/250 sec, f/2.8, ISO 640, 85mm
Lisa Warninger

[2] Good Will Bunting
Canon EOS 50D
1/250 sec, f/3.2, ISO 100, 50mm
Heidi Adnum

[3] Vanilla and Poppy Seed Letter Soaps
Canon EOS 1D MkII
1/30 sec, f/2.5, ISO 400, 100mm
Bill Bradshaw

[4] Wayfarer Pack
Canon Digital Rebel T1i
1/50 sec, f/5.6, ISO 200, 55mm
LAYERxlayer

Exposure

Exposure is the total amount of light received by the camera's sensor and is determined primarily by the aperture and shutter settings. It can affect many elements of an image, including its color, focus, and detail. Similar to managing light, balance is the key to getting it right.

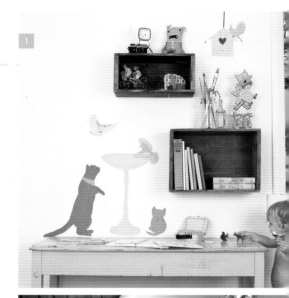

The other factor that affects exposure is the ISO setting. The photographic ISO system was established to determine standards for the speed of light-sensitive film (also referred to as ASA) and the ISO of a digital camera refers to its sensitivity in relation to its film equivalent. A digital camera's sensitivity depends on the size and type of its sensor. Adjusting the ISO makes the sensor more or less sensitive to light and increases or decreases the exposure. The lower the ISO, the less sensitive the sensor is to light, and vice versa. As the ISO increases, the sensor works harder, and if the ISO increases to a level that the sensor struggles with, "noise" or "grain" can be seen on the photograph, making it look less clear or like little gray dots. It's best to keep the ISO as low as possible. ISO cannot be controlled on the automatic setting.

There is a smart feature on many digital cameras that automatically adjusts exposure and is often called "exposure compensation." You instruct the camera to deliberately over- or underexpose the image. This is a helpful tool if the ambient light is much lighter or darker than the light on your product, as many cameras will try to adjust the exposure of an image based on the overall amount of light received.

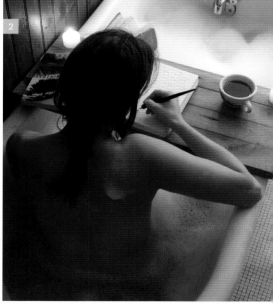

[1] Reusable Fabric Wall Decal
Canon EOS 30D
1/125 sec, f/5.6,
ISO 100, 50mm
Mae

[2] Bathtub Caddy
Nikon D80
1/8 sec, f/3.8,
ISO 400, 28mm
Peg and Awl

THE HISTOGRAM

Reading the histogram is the key to learning more about your exposure. The histogram is a graph showing the balance of light in an image. If you can't find it, refer to your camera manual. If your camera doesn't offer a histogram in the display menu, you can look out for it in your editing program.

The histogram shows the distribution of brightness values in a photograph from black/dark on the left to white/light on the right; all other levels (the "midtones") are shown in the middle of the graph. The height of the vertical peaks represents the number of pixels for each brightness value in the image. Spikes at the very ends represent "blown-out" or "burned" areas where detail has been lost and all that shows is pure white or pure black. Photographing pure black or white or sun flare makes it difficult to avoid spikes at the end(s). The shape of the curve or spikes will vary from image to image and there is no right or wrong—a beautiful photograph can still have an unbalanced histogram. What is important is that you understand the basics of a histogram as that will help you gauge exposure.

UNDERSTANDING THE HISTOGRAM

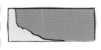

A dark, moody, or under-exposed image will be weighted to the left of the histogram.

A light, bright, or over-exposed image will be weighted to the right of the histogram.

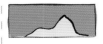

An image with a balance of light and dark areas without any pure white or black will appear more toward the center of the histogram.

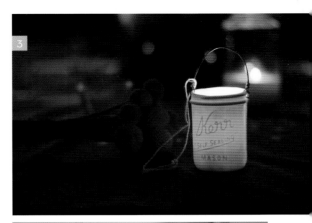

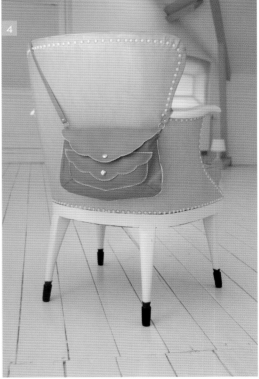

[3] Kerr Votive Lantern
Canon EOS 20D
1/100 sec, f/1.8,
ISO 1600, 50mm
Alicia Carrier

[4] Johanna Handbag
Nikon D70
1/30 sec, f/4.2,
ISO 400, 29mm
Eveline de Heij

Color

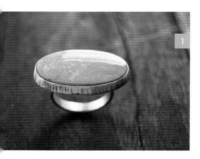

You've put a lot of effort into getting the color of your product just right and you want to show it off. Displaying accurate and vivid color will please customers, as they'll know what they're going to get, and also the media who are looking for images that jump off the page. So, it's important to get it right.

Problems with color are almost always the result of under- or overexposure, incorrect white-balance setting, and/or color-cast. If your photograph appears to have a gray tint, then it is probably underexposed. If it has lost detail and the lighter colors seem to have blended into other areas, then it is probably overexposed. To fix over- or underexposure you need to shift away from the automatic settings and look at the aperture, shutter, and ISO settings. You can also try using exposure compensation (see page 20). The color temperature (or white-balance setting) tells the camera what is pure white. If the camera gets white right, then all the other colors, including skin-tone, will follow.

White balance is largely based on the knowledge that different types of light are either warmer or cooler. It is measured, expressed, and corrected along the Kelvin (K) scale of measurement, with cooler colors represented by larger numbers and warmer colors by smaller numbers. For example, cloudy skies (6000K) are cooler than midday sun (5500K) and midday sun is cooler than sunset/sunrise (3000K). A photograph that appears too blue, orange, or green has the wrong white balance. Many digital cameras have a range of preset white-balance levels to help you get it right without

having to set the Kelvin value yourself. Some digital cameras also allow you to manually reset the white balance, usually by photographing a white or gray sheet of paper (or manually entering a Kelvin value).

Using two or more sources of light is very confusing to the camera. For example, if you have turned on a household lamp (3000K) and also a fluorescent overhead light (4000K) you are mixing colors and creating a color-cast. No matter how many times you change the white balance, the color will never be quite right. This is because no single white-balance setting is correct when there is more than one source of light. Avoid this by using only one light source and use its corresponding preset balance setting.

As light falls onto your scene, it bounces on and off objects, such as the background and your product. If you are using a strongly colored background, you may see a color-cast over your product in the photograph. Avoid this by moving your product further away from the background, or by using a neutral background.

This can all sound scary and confusing, but don't worry—if you stick to one source of light (e.g., natural light) you shouldn't have any problems.

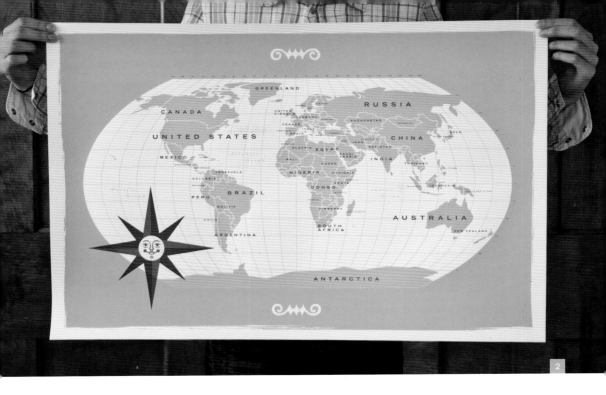

There are also factors that affect color presentation in a photograph that have nothing to do with lighting or camera settings. These include monitor display differences and image compression. We'll talk more about these in Section III.

[1] Simplicity Ring
Nikon D40X
5/300 sec, f/5.6, ISO 360, 55mm
Society Hill Designs

[2] Modern World Map
Canon Rebel XSi
1/60 sec, f/3.2, ISO 200, 35mm
These Are Things

[3] Frenchie Clutch
Canon 5D MkII
1/160 sec, f/8, ISO 160, 59mm
Craig VanDerSchaegen

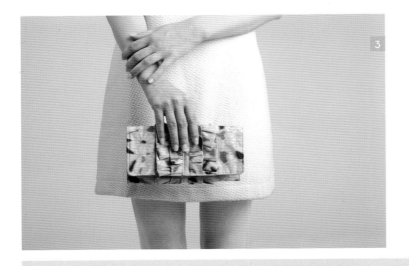

Flash is daylight-balanced at around 5500K, so is OK to use in combination with natural light.

Focus

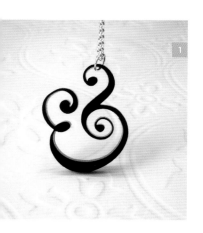

Focus is the clarity and definition of an image. How much of your image is in focus is up to you (and your aperture setting), but for product photography it is essential that at least one part is in sharp focus.

There is a difference between photographs that have deliberate blur or motion, or a "soft-focus" effect, and those that are simply out of focus. In creative or fine art photography, soft focus or blur is a popular technique used to express motion, fluidity, or emotion (amongst other things). When you are trying to sell a product, however, you must make your photograph as clear as possible, so that your customers can see what they're going to get.

The most common factors that affect focus are light and movement. If your scene is too dark or too bright, the camera will have trouble locating the object and, therefore, will find it difficult to focus. You will also lose focus if your camera or subject moves as you take the photograph. If your photograph is out of focus:

→ Delete it and try again. No amount of post-processing can fully recover an out-of-focus photograph to the level required for product photography, so it's important to get it right in the first place. The editing tool "sharpening" shouldn't be confused with focus (more on page 150).

→ Check the distance between the lens and your product, as it may be too close.
→ If your camera has the prefocus option, use it by gently pressing down the shutter to halfway before taking the photograph. This gives the camera time to align the lens and focus on the point selected.
→ Place your camera on a stable surface (or use a tripod) and use the timer to ensure the camera is still when the shutter is activated.
→ Check the focal point that your lens is using. You may be using a point that is picking up detail behind or beside your intended point of focus. The focal point cannot usually be changed on full-automatic mode.
→ Check the camera battery. Low charge can affect overall performance of the camera.
→ If you are using a DSLR and lens that allows for manual focus, try it out. Manually focusing a lens can help with close-up shots, or with objects that have various points on which the camera could focus.

[1] Ampersand Necklace
Sony DSC-P200
1/80 sec, f/5.6, ISO 100, 7.9mm
Jennifer Putzier

[2] Helvetica Bear Letterpress Card
Canon Digital Rebel XTi
1/320 sec, f/11, ISO 400, 28mm
Letterpress Delicacies

[3] Leather Luggage Tag
Nikon D3000
1/600 sec, f/5.3, ISO 250, 42mm
Brandy Murphy

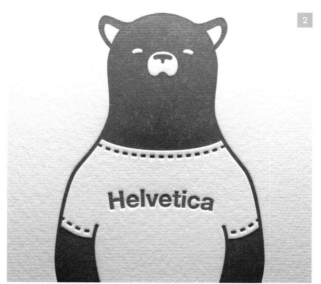

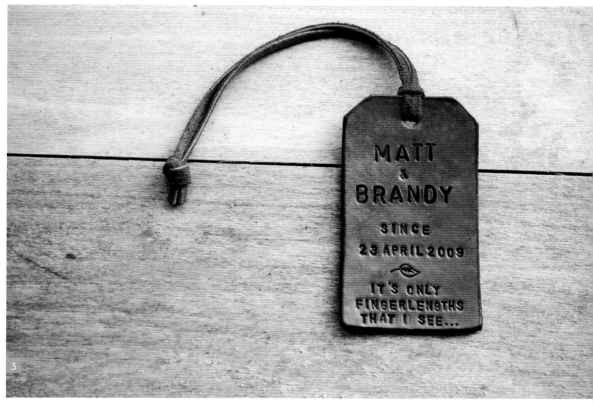

Choosing a Digital Camera

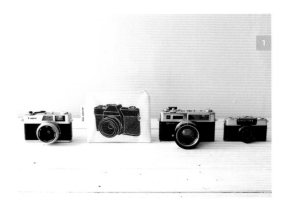

Shopping for a digital camera can be overwhelming: There are so many features and terms that it's easy to become confused. Browse through the following features and extras and develop your own short list of what you really want—it can help to narrow down your options and weed out the timewasters. We'll consider the two main options that you have: digital compact or digital single-lens reflex (DSLR).

RESOLUTION (OR MEGAPIXELS)

Digital images are made up of very small dots called pixels and each pixel contains information about the color of an object. A megapixel equals one million pixels, so, the more megapixels a digital camera has, the more pixels its sensor can detect. This means a camera with more megapixels can produce a more detailed (and possibly better quality) image. The number of megapixels an image contains is also a determinant of the maximum size at which that image can be printed. (See page 156 for more information on resolution.)

More megapixels doesn't necessarily mean a camera is better, though. This is largely due to all the other factors that affect image quality, such as lens quality. So, keep resolution in mind, but don't upgrade for more megapixels alone, unless you really need them.

LENS FEATURES

The main features of a lens are its aperture and its ability to zoom. Lenses have an aperture range and the aperture value that you will see advertised will either give you the entire range or the largest aperture of the range. Lenses with large apertures are referred to as "fast" lenses because they open up more widely and, therefore, allow for fast shooting in low-light conditions.

The ability to zoom is referred to as optical zoom in digital compact cameras and focal length in DSLRs. This is the distance between the lens and the sensor when the lens is focused on a point. For compacts, it is displayed as a multiple, e.g., 3x, and in DSLRs in millimeters, e.g., 100mm lens. The larger the focal length, or the greater the optical zoom, the further away from your product you can be when you photograph it.

The resolution of a digital camera is expressed in megapixels and it affects the quality and size of your photographs.

[1] Friends of Film
Pentax K10-D
1/6 sec, f/11,
ISO 400, 28mm
Slide Sideways

[2] Vanilla and Poppy Seed Letter Soaps
Canon EOS 1D MkII
1/4 sec, f/6.3,
ISO 400, 105mm
Bill Bradshaw

In compact cameras, optical zoom is important because it means that the lens in the camera moves. When you zoom in to get closer to your product, optical zoom allows all the pixels on the camera's sensor to be used in the final photograph. Optical zoom is a must, but how much you should look for will be dependent on how much you need to zoom in on your product, and the same applies when buying a new lens for a DSLR. It's safe to ignore digital zoom values altogether, as that's just the measure of how much the camera can magnify and crop down an image during processing. This results in a loss of detail/pixels and a lower quality picture and is not really helpful in product photography.

Do you need more capacity for zoom or better performance in low light? The answer to this will help you determine whether you should go for a camera with higher optical zoom or a larger aperture, or both.

[3] Hand-stained Wood Tags
Canon Digital Rebel XS
1/60 sec, f/5,
ISO 400, 40mm
Natalie Jost

[4] Silver Nestegg Necklace
Nikon D40
1/60 sec, f/2.8,
ISO 200, 50mm
Amity Roach

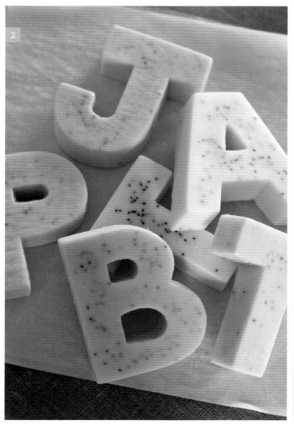

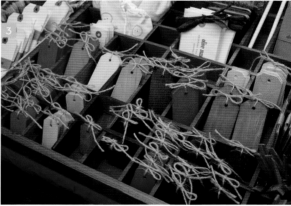

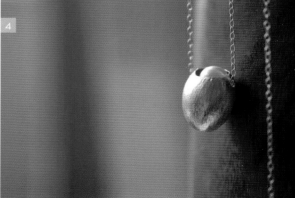

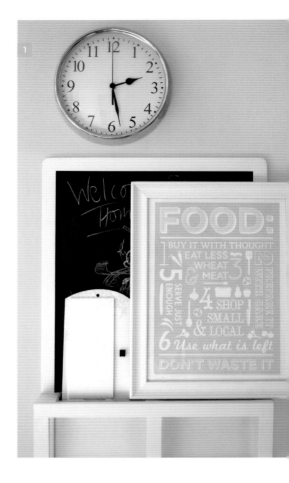

[1] Food Screenprint Poster
Olympus EP-1
1/13 sec, f/2.8, ISO 400, 20mm
Katie Marcus

[2] Puppet Doll
Fuji FinePix s9500
1/15 sec, f/2.8, ISO 400, 6.2mm
Robyn Wilson-Owen

BRANDS

Evaluating different camera brands is a matter of personal preference and experience. If you're unsure, stick to one of the top brands that offers a good warranty and a competitive price.

EXTRA FEATURES

Some added features on digital cameras, such as a large LCD screen and self-timer, are essential for product photography. If the camera doesn't have a traditional viewfinder (many compact cameras do not), you will be relying upon the LCD screen to compose the photograph. If the LCD is too small, you won't be able to see clearly all the details and inclusions in the frame.

Other added features are highly desirable but are not essential, such as image stabilization or video. Some features, such as the type of storage format or interface to connect the camera to your PC, will be used as selling points, but it's safe to assume that the various different types offered by the leading brands are all going to be acceptable. There are also features that are mentioned as selling points, such as autofocus, but nowadays these are the bare minimum and should be standard on all digital cameras.

And there will always be features that you won't ever use and so are a waste of money. Determining what features these are is an entirely personal decision.

CUSTOMER CARE

Before committing to a camera from any store, whether online or bricks-and-mortar, be aware of their post-purchase customer-care policy. You certainly want a new camera to come with a sturdy manufacturer's warranty, but if something goes wrong with the camera/lens and it needs repairs, you want to be able to return the device to the retailer easily. If you can't walk the camera back into the store or post it to the online retailer at no cost to you, you might have to pay expensive shipping costs and worry about damage in transit that may also be your responsibility. Some retailers may not even deal with repairs, leaving you to contact the manufacturer directly.

TRUSTED REVIEW WEBSITES

Depending on the amount of information they list and their intended audience, review websites like www.dpreview.com can be invaluable. They normally offer an extensive glossary of terms and you can usually compare two or more cameras from different manufacturers, looking at the features that matter to you, such as aperture values and other lens features.

PREVIOUS MODEL

When you've decided on the right type of camera for you, shop around. A great time to do so is when a new model is released (usually every one to two years), as the previous model will then be discounted. The new model should have improved upon the last, but the previous model is usually still a perfectly good camera and should still come with a good warranty.

PRE-LOVED

Consider a second-hand camera to save money. If you're looking for a DSLR, look around for photographers who are upgrading their equipment. They'll probably want to upgrade their accessories, too, so you could score a discounted bag, lens cleaner, and so on.

RENT TO TRY OUT

If you're shopping for a DSLR and just can't decide, or if you don't photograph new products very often, renting a camera could be perfect for you. Renting can be more affordable than buying a large camera outright and you could strike up a deal with your local shop for being a regular renter.

FILM CAMERAS

You may feel that there's no place for a film camera in your photography, product or otherwise. But film cameras can improve your overall photography skills and understanding. You may find that the principles of photography will seem clearer when you're using a more straightforward camera without all the bells and whistles of the digital ones.

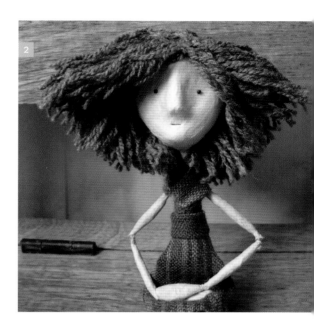

DON'T PAY FOR MORE THAN YOU NEED

It's easy to get caught up in all the little added extras when you're spending a lot of money, but take care to only buy what you need. Take a look at the DIY tutorials in Chapter 3 to work out what accessories you could make yourself or find around the home, rather than paying for them. Don't be afraid to ask for a discount, either, especially if you're about to buy an expensive camera—often retailers will throw in a bag or neck strap as a gesture of thanks—but only if you ask!

MAKE THE MOST OF WHAT YOU HAVE

If you're still unsure about which camera to choose, take some more time to practice with the camera you already have—it may be better than you think. Are there features, buttons, and menu options you've never explored? Have you taken it off automatic and tried it with a tripod? It could save you a load of money. This also applies to the camera you buy, as features that you ignore all add up to a wasted investment.

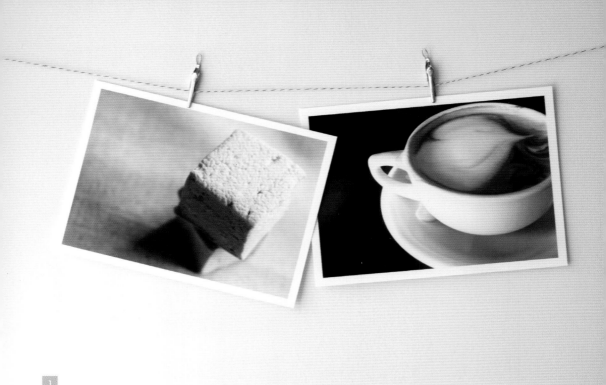

1

DIGITAL COMPACT

These include simple point-and-shoot cameras, standard compacts, and the newer and more comprehensive "enthusiasts' compacts."

Point-and-shoot and standard compacts

Advantages:
→ Mostly small, lightweight, and cheap.
→ Straightforward and easy to use.
→ Some larger standard versions include better sensors for improved image quality.

Disadvantages:
→ Their small design can mean that they lack many features that help to create high-quality images.
→ Built with smaller sensors to keep the price down. Small sensors cannot capture as much detail and are less light-sensitive than large sensors, so the image quality is lower.

→ Can be slow to focus, activate the shutter, and take the photograph.
→ Often no manual function setting, restricting the range of use.
→ Optical zoom could be limited or nonexistent.
→ No interchangeable lens.
→ Can run on standard batteries, making recharging expensive or a battery charger and rechargeable batteries essential.

Suitable for crafters who:
→ are on a strict budget;
→ shoot in well-lit areas.

[1] Coffee and Marshmallows
Canon Digital Rebel T1i
1/64 sec, f/3.5, ISO 100, 50mm
Sweet Fine Day

Digital Smartphones may not be suitable for full-time product photographs, but, if combined with plenty of soft natural light and stability, they could tide you through until you've saved for a new camera.

Enthusiasts' compacts

Advantages:

→ Smaller, lighter, and some are cheaper than DSLR cameras.
→ Contain larger sensors than point-and-shoot cameras, resulting in higher quality images.
→ Should include a higher quality lens than standard compacts.
→ Generally faster than point-and-shoot cameras.
→ Some have interchangeable lenses.

Disadvantages:

→ Larger and heavier than point-and-shoot cameras.
→ The latest models can be more expensive than some entry-level DSLRs.
→ Their sensors are often smaller than that of DSLRs, so the image quality is not quite as good.

Suitable for crafters who:

→ are looking for more than a point-and-shoot but who know they won't use all the features of a DSLR;
→ struggle with low-light conditions and/or who need higher quality images for print;
→ photograph small items that require sharp focus;
→ need larger images for print.

DIGITAL SINGLE LENS REFLEX (DSLR)

Advantages:

→ Contain a large sensor, resulting in higher quality images.
→ Allow you to look through the lens to take the photograph.
→ Offer full control over every setting on your camera, as well as full-automatic and semi-automatic settings.
→ Can use higher ISO levels to increase light sensitivity without causing as much noise or grain as a compact camera.
→ Interchangeable lenses, meaning they are very adaptable in various light conditions.
→ Generally faster than other cameras to focus, activate the shutter, and take the photograph.

Disadvantages:

→ Larger, heavier, and more expensive than compacts.
→ Packed full of features that are included in the price but can often go unused.
→ Require maintenance and cleaning.

Suitable for crafters who:

→ want to improve their photography skills;
→ are constantly working in low-light conditions;
→ wish to use and have more control over DoF;
→ photograph very small items that require fine, ultra-sharp focus;
→ want to use a specialized low-light lens;
→ need large images for print.

Getting to Know Your Camera

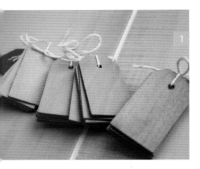

Most photographic challenges can be met, if not overcome altogether, by improving technique; this comes from effort and practice. Bigger and better equipment can help to make things easier, but it's not essential. Regardless of whether your camera is new or old, compact or DSLR, the first and the most important thing you can actually do to improve your photography is to read the manual and move away from the automatic setting. Preset and semi-automatic modes and settings are designed to make a better photograph under certain conditions, such as low light or close range. They also give you the flexibility to allow in more or less light and to control the look of your photograph.

Reading the manual might sound boring, but you need to know what your camera will and won't do. You don't have to read it all at once—that's far too much information: go through the basics first. If you're unsure about the terminology contained within, refer to the Glossary on page 182.

A good habit to get into is to quickly run through the camera settings before you start shooting. This will help to minimize mistakes such as shooting on small-size/low-quality mode when you should be shooting on full-size/high-quality mode.

Visit the website of your camera's manufacturer, as they probably offer a treasure trove of information to help you get the most out of their cameras. Also visit www.youtube.com where many photographers (professional and amateur) offer free online video tutorials, which can be very specific and might help you to overcome particular challenges.

Choose something that you really love and practice shooting that—your family, pets, food, home, or even your product—it doesn't matter. As long as you love it, you're more likely to do it and to learn from it. Shoot at different times of the day and in different light conditions to get a feel for the result it has on your photographs. And, if it doesn't work first time around, be patient and persevere.

[1] Hand-stained Wood Gift Tags
Canon PowerShot S2 IS
1/60 sec, f/5, ISO 400, 40mm
Natalie Jost

[2] Woody Allen Print
Canon PowerShot SX110 IS
1/125 sec, f/2.8, ISO 400, 78mm
Judy Kaufmann

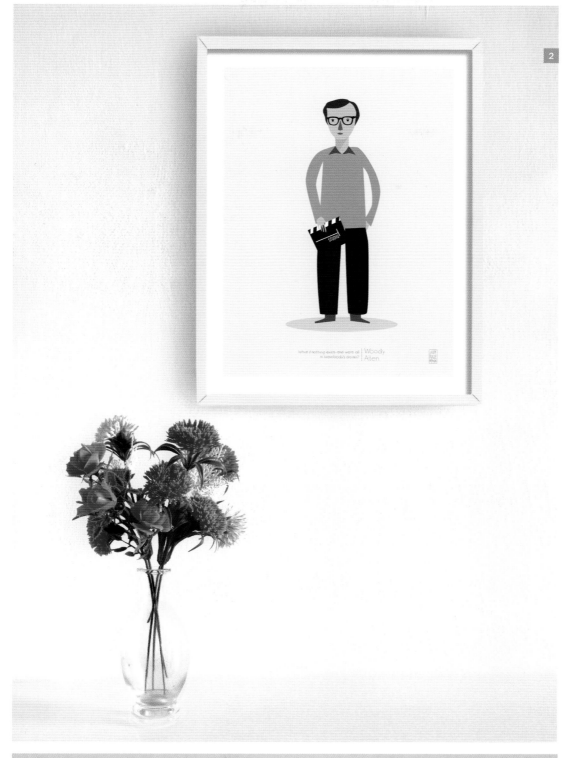

Major Digital Camera Modes

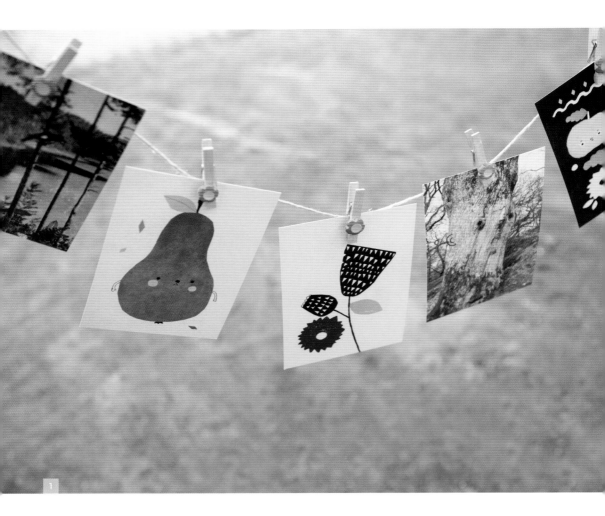

[1] Postcards
Canon EOS 5D
1/60 sec, f/4, ISO 320, 38mm
Fine Little Day

Modes and settings range from camera to camera and the settings overlap; some digital compacts also offer manual settings, and DSLRs offer preset modes. They are all about allowing more or less light into the camera.

PRESET/SEMI-AUTOMATIC

→ **Automatic** uses a built-in light sensor to gauge the amount of ambient light and set all levels, including flash. User usually has no control over any setting.

→ **Portrait** uses a mid-range aperture to create moderate DoF and so a slightly blurry background.

→ **Landscape** uses a small aperture to create a larger DoF and hence a more in-focus foreground and background. The aim is to keep as much detail in the photograph in focus as possible.

→ **Macro** uses a large aperture to create a shallow DoF and blur the background. Instructs the camera to focus on an object near to the lens.

→ **Nighttime** uses a high ISO and slower shutter speed to allow in more light into the camera, often using built-in flash.

→ **Action/kids** uses the highest possible shutter speed and ISO to take fast images that capture movement. Normally without using built-in flash. To compensate for such a fast shutter speed, the aperture is usually very large, resulting in a blurred background.

SEMI-AUTOMATIC

→ **P/Program** uses a preset value for aperture and shutter speed based on a reading of the light meter. Allows the user to set other features like the ISO, white balance, point of focus, as well as turn the flash off or on.

→ **A/Aperture Priority/Av/Aperture Value** allows the user to determine the aperture value and the camera calculates the shutter and sometimes the ISO settings.

→ **S/Shutter Priority/Tv/Time Value** allows the user to determine the shutter (or time) value and the camera calculates the aperture and sometimes the ISO settings.

MANUAL

→ **M/Manual** allows the user to determine the aperture value, shutter speed, ISO, and various other settings.

See the Glossary on page 182 for other common settings.

Planning Your Photograph

You've read up on the fundamentals of photography and have your camera ready to go. What you need to do next is to plan your photograph in order to work out what kind of look you want.

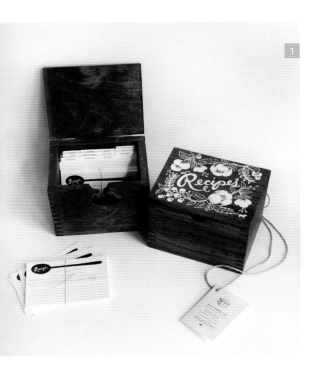

[1] Heirloom Recipe Box
Nikon D80
1/35 sec, f/4.5, ISO 200, 40mm
Rifle Paper Co.

If you're not sure what photographic style you most like or even where to start, take a look around for inspiration. Get an account on www.flickr.com and create a list of favorites. You can do the same on www.etsy.com and other popular photographic or craft websites. Join www.tumblr.com or browse your favorite blogs and catalogs. Revisit the products you have been inspired to buy. You'll soon see what kinds of photograph you are drawn to. Developing your own style can be fun and creative, but if it becomes frustrating, you're probably thinking about it too much. Remember, you don't have to do something that's never been done before—simple is often best.

It's very important to take the time to clean/tidy up your product before shooting, especially for the detail shots where every piece of dust or fluff and every fingerprint may show.

Remember your goals and the story you want your product and brand to tell. Try to convey your passion and enthusiasm for your product and what sets your product apart from your competitors.

Experimenting will help you to find the right style of photographs for your product. Once you've found what works, try to stick with it. Consistency sends many positive messages to your customers, including that your business and products have

Treat fads and trends with a sense of humor. Have fun with them but don't feel that you need to follow them. Practice, experiment, and develop your own style.

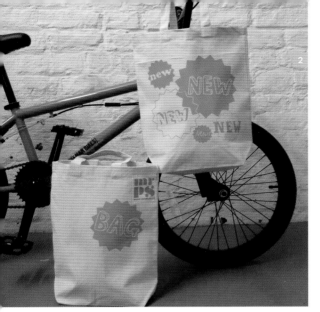

a clear purpose and direction. Achieve consistency by using the same background and/or lighting for every photograph. Your photographs will also look great together and that may have your customers buying more than one or having fun deciding which ones they love most.

Consistency doesn't mean you have to keep the same photographs forever, nor does it mean every photograph has to be exactly the same. But when you're looking at a collection of photographs, all the differences stand out. If you're changing your photographs, or have improved your style, take the time to reshoot the older ones, too, if possible. If you try to keep the basic features the same, then what will stand out will be the subtle differences between each product, which is what you want.

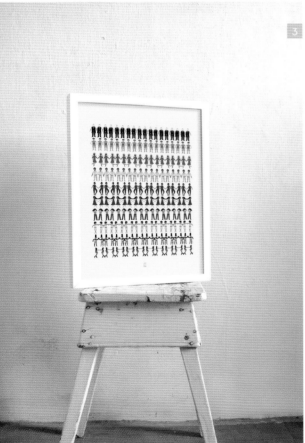

[1] Heirloom Recipe Box
Nikon D80
1/35 sec, f/4.5, ISO 200, 40mm
Rifle Paper Co.

[2] New Bag
Panasonic DMC-FS6
1/25 sec, f/2.8, ISO 400, 5.5mm
Megan Price

[3] People Print
Canon PowerShot SX110 IS
1/125 sec, f/2.8, ISO 400, 78mm
Judy Kaufmann

Composition

Composing your photograph is about taking all the separate parts—product, lighting, background, props—and bringing them together to form one cohesive and clear message. The ultimate goal of composing your photograph should be to make it as appealing to the eye as possible, generating interest in your product and drawing in your customer.

ORIENTATION

Usually the first decision you make when composing your photograph is if you're going to shoot in portrait/vertical or landscape/horizontal orientation. This is often determined by where you are going to display your photograph (e.g., a website or magazine) and your/their requirements for shape, size, and so on. If you plan on cropping your photograph into a square later on, compose and shoot in portrait/vertical orientation, as the sides become your guide for the width of the square.

FRAMING

When you look through the viewfinder or the LCD screen to position your camera and lens, you are framing your photograph. It is called framing because it's exactly like adding a physical frame to the scene to trim down information and eliminate distractions.

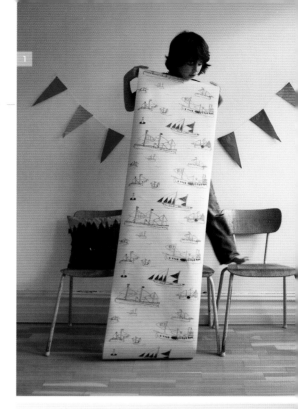

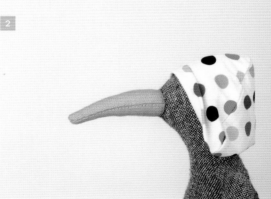

When you buy a photo frame, you fill it with the right size photograph—use this principle when framing the shot and make the most of the frame.

CROPPING OUT DISTRACTIONS

Distracting elements

Distractions can be objects that appear in the image but don't serve any useful purpose or prove a point. Even a change between indoors and outdoors, such as sky above a roof, can be a distraction.

Cropping out distractions

Eliminating distractions is an important part of framing and this will come naturally to you when you start to fill the entire frame with meaningful information, or deliberate blank space. Sometimes you have to take one photograph to see the full extent of what your lens has captured in the frame (you can always delete it afterward—the ability to do this has to be one of the greatest advantages of digital photography). Look for areas where your scene drops off, such as the edge of a table or the side of a backdrop. Look for bits and pieces that have made their way into the frame that don't need to be there and remove them or recompose so that you can no longer see them.

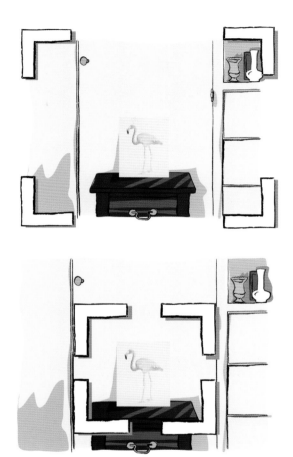

[1] **Ohoy Wallpaper**
Canon EOS 5D
1/60 sec, f/4,
ISO 320, 38mm
Fine Little Day

[2] **Rare Species
of a Bird**
Canon PowerShot S11
1/125 sec, f/2.8,
ISO 400, 78mm
Hagar Cygler

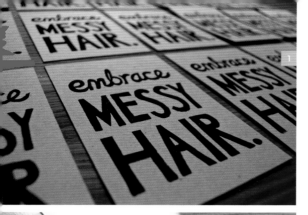

[1] Embrace Messy Hair Lino Print
Nikon D40
1/80 sec, f/4.5, ISO 800, 19mm
Funnelcloud Studio

[2] Handmade Rubber Stamp
Nikon D3000
1/160 sec, f/6.3, ISO 2000, 105mm
Mollie Flatley

[3] E for Egg Alphabet Ceramic Plate
Canon Digital Rebel XSi
1/250 sec, f/4.5, ISO 200, 50mm
Just Noey

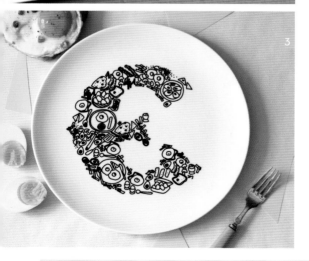

DIRECTION AND VIEWPOINT

Remember that the direction from which you shoot your product will be your customer's viewpoint. If you select an unusual crop or a particular detail and use this as your headline image, your customers will be intrigued!

→ Grouping your products together can make them more eye-catching. This is especially true for small items.
→ Framing your photograph in the camera first is a good habit to get into and will save you time and hassle cropping later on.
→ Shoot from above to show your product in its entirety, especially if it is large in size or an awkward shape. Use a stepladder if necessary. This is a good way to fit the product and props into one frame.
→ Shoot from below to add drama to your photograph, enhance its sense of humor or make it look bigger.
→ Shoot straight-on to make your product look bold and impressive, connecting it to your customer by putting it at eye-level: It's like making eye-contact.

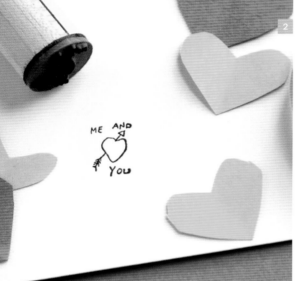

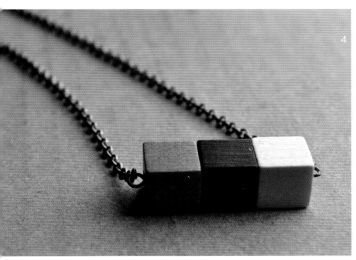

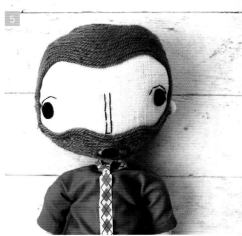

RULES

There are formal rules for the composition of photographs (and other forms of visual art), but they should be treated more as a fundamental guide than a series of rights and wrongs. These include the rule of thirds, leading lines, and center of interest, and are all fairly straightforward—see the Glossary on page 182 for more information.

[4] Triple Cube Necklace
Nikon D90
1/60 sec, f/8, ISO 220, 40mm
Little O by wolfbrother

[5] Handmade Doll
Nikon D40
1/40 sec, f/3.5, ISO 400, 18mm
Simpli Jessi

[6] Footed Platter
Nikon D80
1/50 sec, f/5.3, ISO 400, 75mm
Elizabeth Bryant

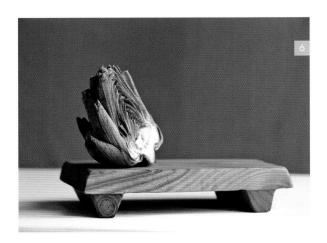

Choosing Backgrounds

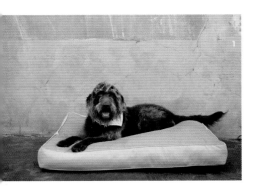

Backgrounds can be wonderfully simple and easy to work with. The right background has the potential to ensure your product is the first thing customers notice when they look at your photograph.

Once you've found the right background, stick with it—this is a great way to create consistency and encourage your customers to browse your product range.

Alternating between different backgrounds can be distracting. Using the same flattering background for all of your photographs creates a sense of cohesion, style, and organization.

Whilst your photographs need to look good together, they also need to look good on their own. Look at one of your photographs as if it were standing alone in a magazine feature or on a blog and question whether that one image tells your brand story.

Most backgrounds fall into at least one of the following five categories: neutral, colored, textured, patterned, or in situ.

Neutral

If you are in any doubt as to which background will best suit your product, always go for a neutral background. They are the simplest and often the most effective. Neutral backgrounds look very refined and professional, and will suit every product. They can be any shade of white, gray, or black.

Pure white and jet black may sound like the perfect neutral backgrounds but they are very harsh on the eye and the high contrast can be unflattering for your product, so you're best to stick to softened white or black.

White backgrounds are perfect for a minimalist effect and they are easily found or made—walls, fabrics, a light tent, or a seamless background (see Chapter 3).

[1] Southern Palms
X-Large Dog Bed
Canon EOS 5D Mk2
1/80 sec, f/3.5, ISO 160, 55mm
Kristen Beinke Photography

[2] Dinosaur Card
Olympus E-420
1/40 sec, f/4.1, ISO 400, 20mm
Pawling Print Studio

[3] Acid House
Nikon D700
1/10 sec, f/8, ISO 100, 60mm
Alan Tansey

[4] Polka
Nikon D700
1/8 sec, f/8, ISO 100, 60mm
Alan Tansey

[5] Folk
Nikon D700
1/8 sec, f/8, ISO 100, 60mm
Alan Tansey

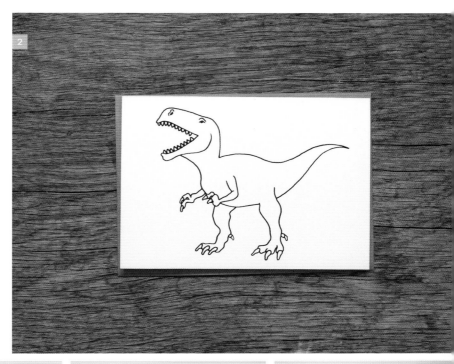

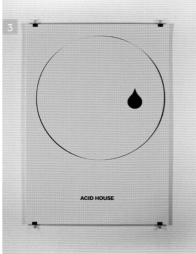

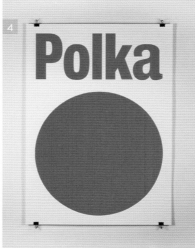

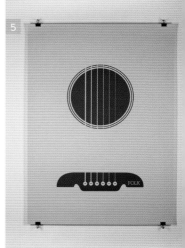

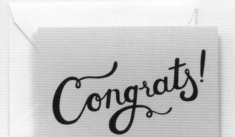

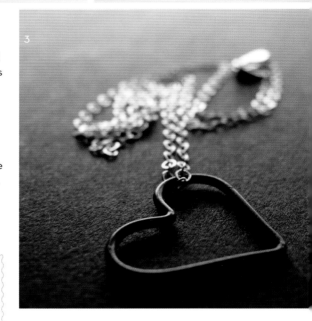

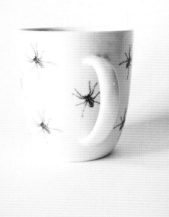

Even white or pale products can look great on a white background. The effect is very airy, crisp, and clean, and is a technique often employed by stylists to convey high quality and modern simplicity.

The best way to use black is to choose an "almost" black background, like charcoal or dark gray using paper, tiles, fabric, blackboards, painted MDF board, or stained wood. Darker backgrounds create more of a mood, so best suit strong, bold products. If your product is dark in color, then don't rule out an almost-black background.

If you're unhappy with the color of your wall, then why not change it? Paint a section of the wall (you can always paint it back) or, if that isn't possible, paint a piece of MDF and slide it into the background.

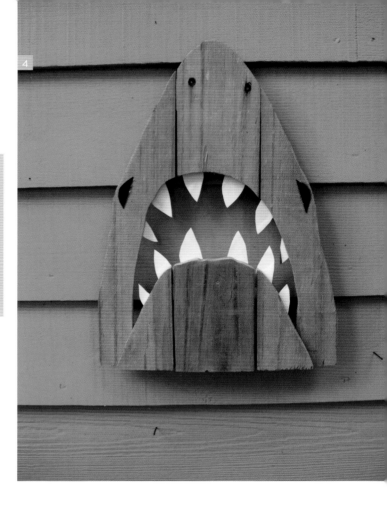

If you're unsure what colors would best suit your products, pick up a paint chart that includes the color(s) of your product. You will then have an example of similar colors of the same shade.

[1] Screenprinted Congrats Card
Nikon D80
1/35 sec, f/4.5, ISO 200, 50mm
Rifle Paper Co.

[2] Blue Bugs Mug
Canon PowerShot G10
1/60 sec, f/2.8, ISO 200, 24mm
Bailey Doesn't Bark

[3] One Dark Heart
Sony Cyber-Shot DSC-H3
1/40 sec, f/3.5, ISO 250, 6.3mm
Lauren Haupt Estes

[4] Shark Made of Recycled Fence Wood
Kodak EasyShare C813
1/60 sec, f/2.7, ISO 120, 6mm
John Birdsong

Colored

Colored backgrounds are versatile and can really make an impact. They range from very delicate and sweet pastels, which create a soft and dreamy effect, to stronger colors for a fun, bold effect.

A colored surface, such as a laminated tabletop or wall, is great as a background, or make your own from paper or fabric. Tape paper to the wall and drape it down onto the floor or table—just remember to select a matte, non-shine paper. If you'd like to try a colored background but don't think bright colors or pastels would suit, experiment with brown paper.

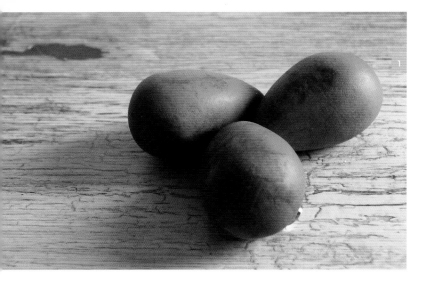

[1] Robin's Egg Magnets
Kodak Easyshare C743
1/25 sec, f/2.7, ISO 160, 6mm
Jennifer Arndt

[2] Lined Paper Card
Nikon D300
1/500 sec, f/5.6, ISO 250, 35mm
Erin Riley

[3] Ants on My Card Set
Canon PowerShot G10
1/40 sec, f/2.8, ISO 400, 24mm
Bailey Doesn't Bark

Textured

Textured backgrounds, such as wood, bricks, fabric, and paper, are a real treat to work with and can nicely complement your product. Textured backgrounds will also fall into one of the other categories; e.g., charcoal-colored paper is a textured and neutral background.

Wood is one of the cheapest and most effective textured backgrounds and works like a neutral to suit almost every product.

Fabric is a great choice for backgrounds and its interesting but fine and subtle texture contrasts nicely with metallic products.

Unless you are going for a rustic look, it's very important to keep fabric firm and flat (and always without any stains or tears). If you shoot at home, look around for fabrics that have already been pulled flat and firm, such as chairs, cushions, or headboards. For a more permanent and portable solution, cover a corkboard with the fabric of your choice.

Use your own product as a textured, complementary background, too.

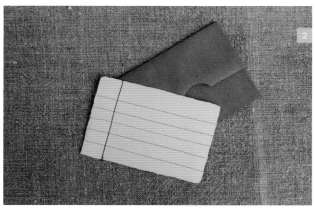

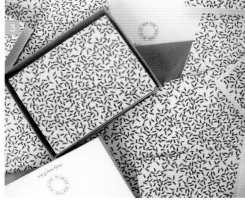

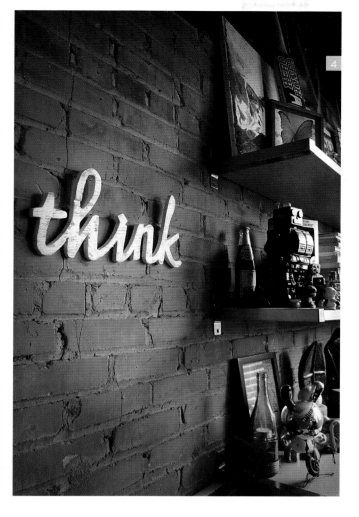

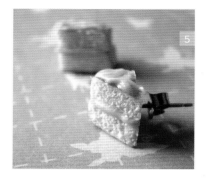

[4] Recycled-wood Think Sign
Panasonic Lumix DMC-LX3
1/40 sec, f/2.2, ISO 320, 28mm
William Dohman

[5] Pink Frosting Cake Slices Earrings
Sony DHC-H7
1/60 sec, f/3.2, ISO 250, 9.7mm
Stéphanie Kilgast

Patterns

Patterns can complement your product nicely.
They can also be difficult to work with. Patterns
that are too loud or dark are distracting and
will swamp your product. The right pattern will
be subtle and will echo the look, feel, and color
of your product. Try non-shine gift wrap or a
tablecloth. Selecting a pattern that includes a
complementary color from your product will tie the
two together nicely and will keep your customers'
focus on the product.

In situ

An in situ background is a superb choice when
you want to inspire customers and suggest to them
ways for how to use your product. Choose locations
in and around your home, garden, or studio.

Props, Styling & Scale

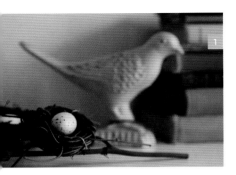

Props are anything in your photograph, aside from the main product, that is used to enhance the scene. Using props is part of styling your photograph, and props and styling can also convey scale—it all works together. The props and styling that you use, along with any references for scale, should always reflect the ethos of your carefully and lovingly handmade product.

Imitation items, such as fake flowers or vintage-look objects, are easy to get hold of but also likely to be mass-produced, made from cheap materials, and not designed to last, and that message takes away from your product.

If your products are roughly the same size but are not exactly the same, e.g., pieces of art or fashion accessories, try to use the same space, crop, and/or perspective for all of your photographs. When your customers view your photographs one after the other or altogether in your online shop, they will be able to see the subtle size differences to then get a sense of scale.

Using your own products and packaging for props is a great way to add value to your photograph and show off more of your range. Your customer knows how you will prepare their purchase and what they should expect.

The best way to show scale is to photograph your product in situ or with a universal reference. If you're using a model, remember that they need to look comfortable and confident while using your product.

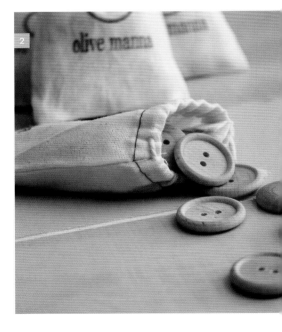

[1] Nests
Nikon D300
1/125 sec, f/4.5,
ISO 640, 55mm
Erin Riley

**[2] Natural
Wood Buttons**
Canon Digital Rebel XS
1/60 sec, f/5.6,
ISO 400, 55mm
Natalie Jost

**[3] Letterpress
Swing Tags**
Canon Digital Rebel XSi
1/400 sec, f/5,
ISO 400, 50mm
Bespoke Letterpress

[4] Rose Fascinator
Canon EOS 5D
1/100 sec, f/5.6,
ISO 200, 55mm
Untamed Petals

[5] Cropped Camisole
Nikon D200
1/100 sec, f/7.1, ISO 100,
50mm
Jo Duck

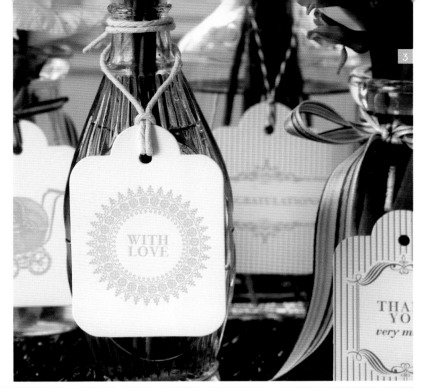

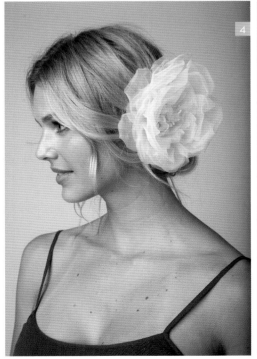

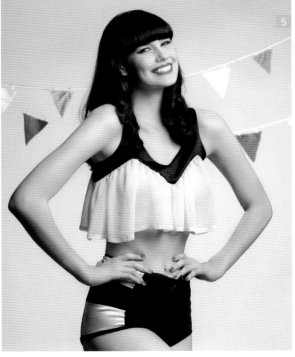

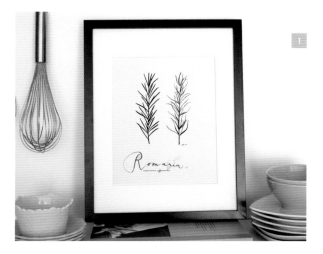

There are a number of universal props and styling techniques that can be used to show scale. These include:

→ items of furniture or home accessories;
→ fresh fruit, vegetables, or flowers, all of which can look superb;
→ books, cotton spools, balloons, potted plants, pencils, or ribbon;
→ styling your product to suggest ways in which to use it; and
→ you can also have some fun setting the scene and creating mood.

If you can't find a prop that both complements your product and shows its scale, consider simply including a beautiful ruler next to your product. You can use that photograph as a supporting image and another, prop-free, for your headlining shot.

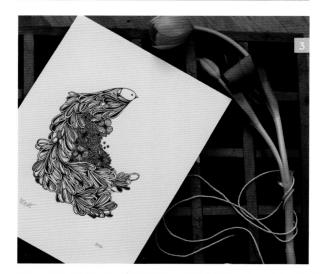

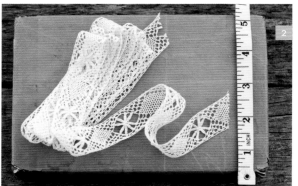

[1] Romarin Print
Nikon E995
1/60 sec, f/2.9, ISO 200, 11mm
Eve Legris

[2] Vintage Lace
Canon EOS 50D
1/100 sec, f/4, ISO 160, 50mm
Heidi Adnum

[3] Letterpress Limited Edition Print
Canon Digital Rebel XSi
1/125 sec, f/3.2, ISO 200, 50mm
Bespoke Letterpress

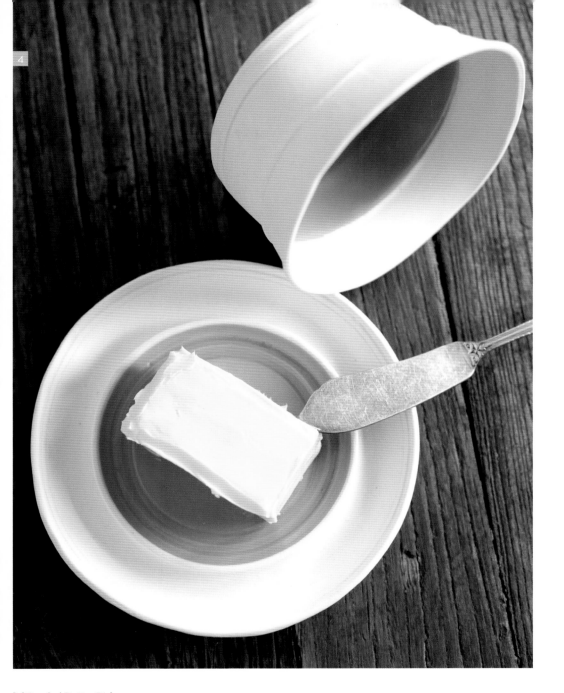

[4] Banded Butter Dish
Nikon D3
1/160 sec, f/3.5, ISO 2000, 50mm
Lisa Warninger

Detail & Texture

To best illustrate texture, get up close to your product
and keep the photograph in sharp focus.

Place your product in a well-lit space and use
a tripod (or equivalent) if you need more stability
to keep the shot in focus. Shoot with your camera
at an angle to your product, or vice versa.

Hard light (such as direct sunlight or undiffused
camera flash) will be too bright and can make
a surface look dull and one-dimensional. Soft,
natural light will fall gently on your product,
highlighting the detail and texture perfectly.

Aim to fill as much of the frame with your product
as possible. A photograph that's full of a small
detail, such as the texture of paper or fabric,
can look very luxurious and conveys a sense
of high quality to your customer.

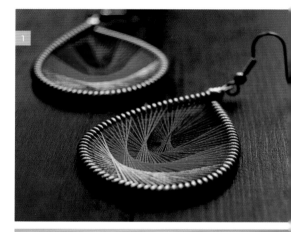

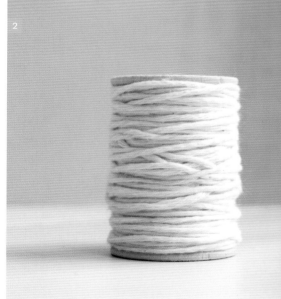

[1] Lima Earrings
Nikon D40
1/125 sec, f/5.6,
ISO 800, 55mm
Three 5 Eighty 5

[2] Natural Cotton Twine
Canon Digital Rebel XS
1/60 sec, f/5.6,
ISO 400, 45mm
Natalie Jost

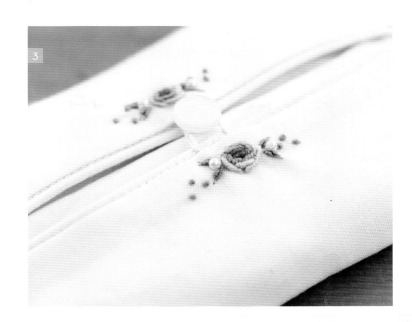

[3] Embroidered Tissue Holder
Canon EOS 50D
1/100 sec, f/3.5, ISO 250, 50mm
Heidi Adnum

**[4] Friendly Dachshund
Dog Collar**
Canon Digital Rebel XS
1/15 sec, f/5.6, ISO 100, 40mm
Silly Buddy

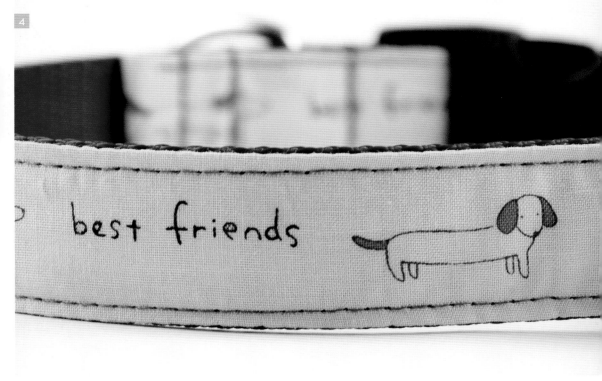

best friends

Light Tent

A light tent is also known as a mini-studio. Light enters the box from above and at the sides, and bounces around inside the box and falls onto your product from many angles. A light tent is a great example of making the light source larger by diffusion and should result in more even exposure and softer shadows. The white background is completely neutral and, subsequently, all focus is placed on the product.

MAKING A LIGHT TENT

As a crafter you'll be delighted to know that while camera-equipment manufacturers make and sell light tents for a range of prices, you can easily make one at home out of a cardboard box and tracing paper. All you need to do is follow these steps.

1. Take a box at least 1ft^2 (30cm^2). Set the box with the opening facing you and cut out the sides and top panel, leaving the back and base intact.

2. Replace the sides and top with semi-transparent white paper (like tracing paper or baking parchment).

3. Create a runway from the back of the box out to the front of the box by taping a sheet of thick, white paper to the top back and draping it down and out the front of the box.

4. Your tent is now ready to be placed near a light source, such as a window or outside, or you can bring light to the tent, such as a lamp or flash.

5. Place your product inside the tent so it is contained within the three-papered walls and shoot.

LIGHTING A LIGHT TENT

You will achieve a well-balanced light within the tent if you position it correctly under the light source. Look at the direction from which the light is entering the tent. If your light source is stacked to one side, e.g., a lamp shining in from the left, you will notice that the right side is slightly darker. If your light is stacked from the top, the sides will be more evenly lit but the shadows underneath your product will be a little darker. To allow in more light to the tent, face it toward another light source, such as a window. If you're finding that the light is not bright enough inside your light tent, consider making an even larger one. Small tents don't allow the light to bounce around as much as larger ones.

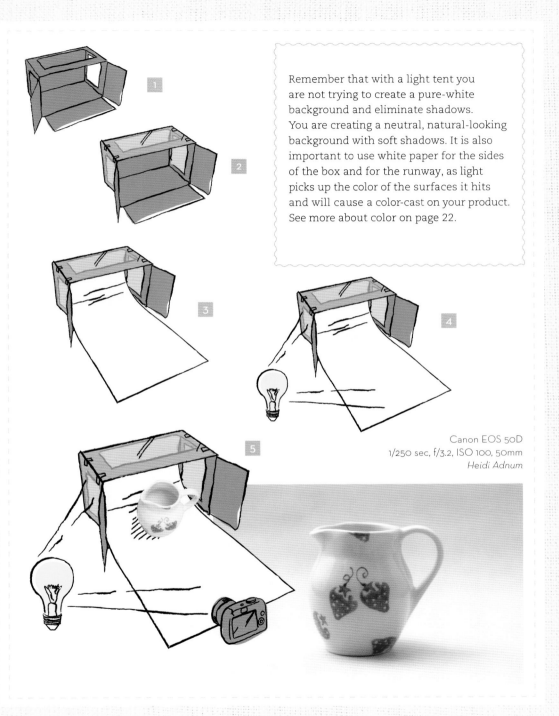

Remember that with a light tent you are not trying to create a pure-white background and eliminate shadows. You are creating a neutral, natural-looking background with soft shadows. It is also important to use white paper for the sides of the box and for the runway, as light picks up the color of the surfaces it hits and will cause a color-cast on your product. See more about color on page 22.

Canon EOS 50D
1/250 sec, f/3.2, ISO 100, 50mm
Heidi Adnum

Light Box

A light box is, quite literally, a box full of lights. Light boxes are a great way to light something from underneath or behind, and have many practical and traditional applications such as viewing slides or x-rays. To make your own light box:

1. Take a plastic container or any kind of sturdy and transparent box that is clear or white in color, and a bundle of white lights, such as fairy lights. You can also use an off-camera flash if you have one or a torch/flashlight.

2. Fill the box with the light source, turn on the light source and replace the lid. If your light source has a cord that needs to be plugged in in order to work but it won't fit underneath the lid of the box, you may have to create a small hole in the box to allow the cord to fit through.

3. If your light box is transparent, you will have to diffuse the light. This is as simple as placing a sheet of paper or fabric over the top.

4. Position your light box near another source of light, such as a window or within a light tent to light the top of the product.

5. We talked about color and white balance on page 22, and how sources of light have their own color. You may need to invest in a daylight-balanced lightbulb to use with your light box if you're struggling with color.

Whether you choose a light tent or light box, either is usually a better alternative than digitally cutting out your product during post-production and placing it onto another with a pure-white background. If you've tried creating a pure-white background in post-production but it just doesn't look right, it's probably because the shadows and finest detail around the edge of the product have been removed during the "select and copy/cut" process. They may seem small and irrelevant, but edges, shadows, and some reflection are very important in showing dimension and depth. When they're taken away, the product can seem somewhat artificial and as though it were strangely hovering in space.

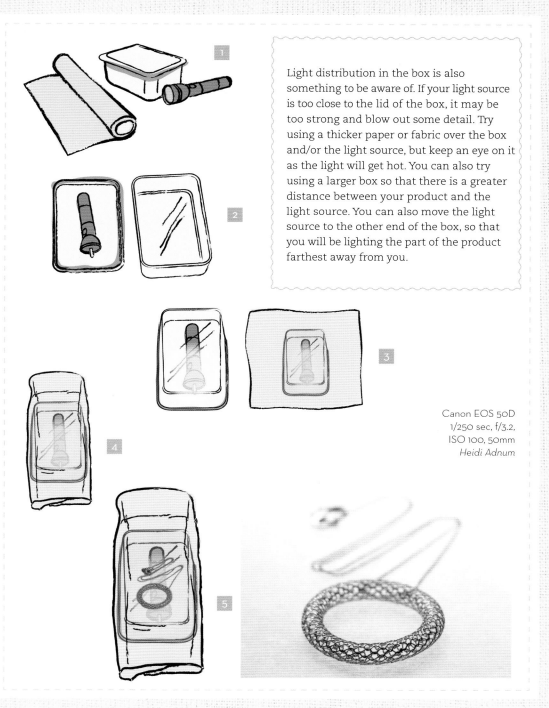

Light distribution in the box is also something to be aware of. If your light source is too close to the lid of the box, it may be too strong and blow out some detail. Try using a thicker paper or fabric over the box and/or the light source, but keep an eye on it as the light will get hot. You can also try using a larger box so that there is a greater distance between your product and the light source. You can also move the light source to the other end of the box, so that you will be lighting the part of the product farthest away from you.

Canon EOS 50D
1/250 sec, f/3.2,
ISO 100, 50mm
Heidi Adnum

Reflector

A reflector is a brilliant way to increase the amount of light available for the camera. The principle is very simple: Use a reflective surface to bounce the light from the main light source onto the object. Reflectors are often used to soften and minimize shadows and to light the other side of the object. They can also provide an alternative to flash when using fill light (see page 15). Photographic product manufacturers often sell white, silver, gold, or black reflectors, but you can easily make your own:

1. Gather a piece of rigid white card stock, some aluminum foil, scissors, and tape.

2. Use either white card as-is, or cover with tin foil and adhere with tape. Cut to size, if necessary. Covering white card with tin foil is not essential but provides a stronger reflection than white card alone. Disposable tin-foil roasting trays or plain mirrors also make good alternatives. White reflectors provide soft and subtle reflected light and silver gives stronger, sometimes even harsh light reflection. Gold is used mainly in portrait photography to provide a flattering warm tone to skin. If you would like to try a gold reflector, pick up a sheet of metallic gold card. Black reflectors are used to add shadows for contour and depth (see page 97).

3. Position the reflector toward the light source and tilt it in the direction of your product. You will notice that the area that you are reflecting light onto becomes lighter and the shadows decrease. If you find that the effect is too strong, switch from a foil reflector to a white card reflector.

Reflectors are ideal for use in conjunction with backlighting and also shooting in shade. If your product is a little too dark in the shade, reflect sunlight onto it. This will be far more effective and becoming than moving the product into the direct sunlight. If you're shooting inside in low light, try reflecting any available window light onto your product.

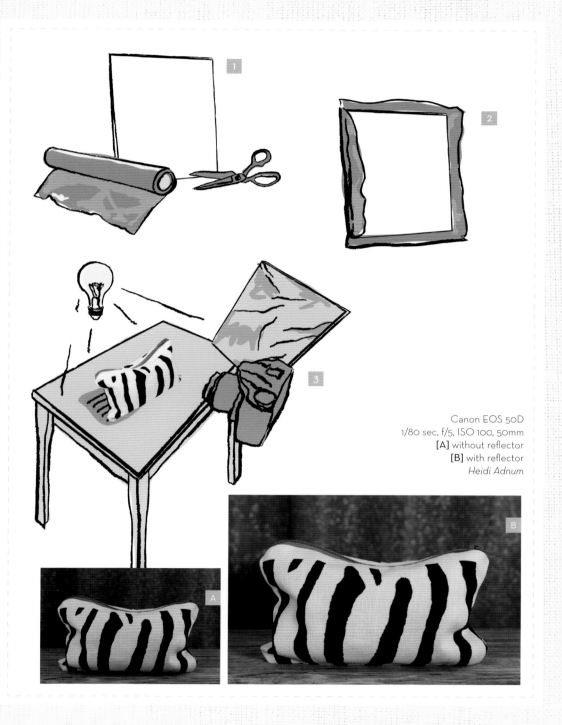

Canon EOS 50D
1/80 sec, f/5, ISO 100, 50mm
[A] without reflector
[B] with reflector
Heidi Adnum

Flash Diffuser

Diffusing flash is a very helpful technique to learn, especially when artificial light is the only way to light a scene. Besides, if flash is already built into your camera, you might as well know how to use it! To diffuse on-camera flash, you can either cover it with a semi-transparent white object or you can redirect it.

Flash is a powerful source of light and will overpower many objects that you cover it with, so when you're perfecting your diffuser, keep trying different white objects until you find the one that works best for your camera. You can start by:

1. Gathering scissors, tape, a pencil, and white paper. What you make your diffuser out of depends on the effect you would like to achieve. For only a small amount of diffusion, a sheet of white paper could do, but it is probably not going to be strong enough to diffuse the flash. For better diffusion, try a thicker piece of white paper or a semi-opaque white plastic, such as coreflute/foamcore.

2. With the camera turned off and the lens protected by its cover, trace around the non-moveable part of the lens.

3. Cut out the hole you have traced.

4. Place the diffuser over the camera and trim to size. The larger you make the diffuser, the larger the light source becomes. You don't have to keep the diffuser to the same size as your camera. Use tape, removable tack, or even small clips to tape the diffuser to the camera. If using a flash diffuser is something you choose to do frequently, you can attach small Velcro dots to your camera and the diffuser for easy attachment. When you attach the diffuser to your camera, be sure not to obscure the lens.

5. When the camera knows it is going to use flash, it can afford to allow in less light through the lens using a faster shutter and/or a smaller aperture, thus decreasing the exposure in lieu of the light the flash will provide. However, the camera doesn't know that you are going to cover or redirect the flash. To compensate for this, you need to "dial up" the exposure compensation. Then, the camera will know to allow in more light, regardless of the on-camera flash it is about to use. It will then adjust to a slower shutter speed or a larger aperture. Read more about exposure compensation on page 20.

To redirect on-camera flash, you need to use a white, opaque object and rest it against the camera under the flash and tilt the card upward. See pages 15 and 105 to see what a redirected flash looks like.

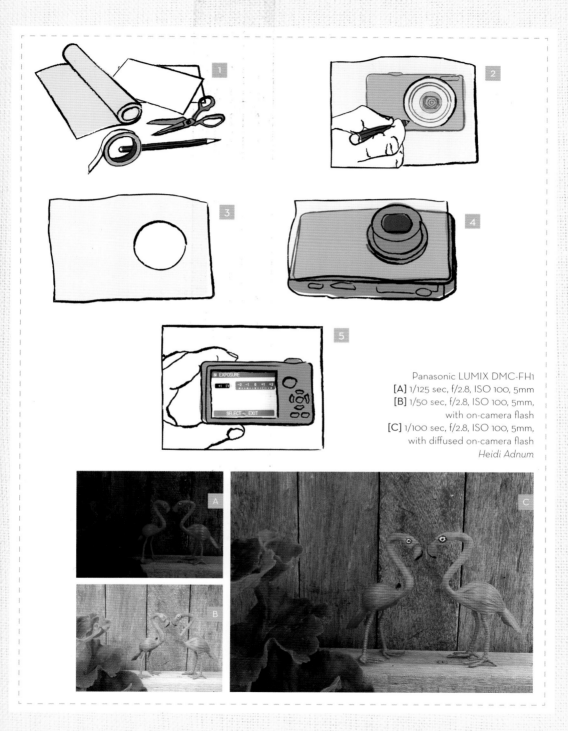

Panasonic LUMIX DMC-FH1
[A] 1/125 sec, f/2.8, ISO 100, 5mm
[B] 1/50 sec, f/2.8, ISO 100, 5mm,
with on-camera flash
[C] 1/100 sec, f/2.8, ISO 100, 5mm,
with diffused on-camera flash
Heidi Adnum

Seamless Background

A seamless background can be an important tool for product photography. White, seamless backgrounds are popular for many types of photography because they don't overpower the subject or cause a color-cast. Normally, seamless backgrounds are expensive and need to be attached to large backdrop frames (also expensive). You can make your own using affordable materials found at home and the local hardware store:

1. A plain white roll of gift wrap is a perfect low-cost and lightweight material to create a seamless background. Another low-cost but larger alternative is a roll of white paper tablecloth. You can also purchase rolls of professional photographic paper at a higher cost if you need the extra width or length. Fabric is also an option. To make a small, seamless background, you'll need your paper, some tape, and tins or weights.

2. Tape the paper to a wall in a well-lit space. Allow the paper to fall gently to the ground, roll it out away from the wall and weigh down the ends.

3. It is important to be gentle when rolling out the paper, as you don't want to tear or crease it. It is also very important to leave a slight curve in the paper and position your product away from the curve. This ensures that the white background looks smooth and seamless.

If you would like to lighten up the white background, you can do so by shining a light directly onto the white paper at the back. The more light you shine onto the white background, the lighter it becomes. This is how to create a high-contrast pure-white background.

If you like the idea of a seamless, white background but would prefer to use backlighting, use tracing paper instead of opaque paper and adhere the paper to a window, not a wall. Window light will shine through the paper and, depending on the intensity of the light and transparency of the paper, may create a light, dreamy, white, studio-background effect. Be aware, though, that if the window is not full-length, a shadow or darker area may appear where the window ends and the rest of the wall begins.

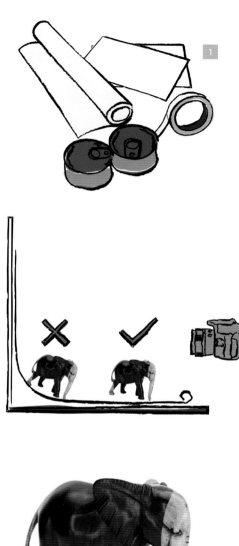

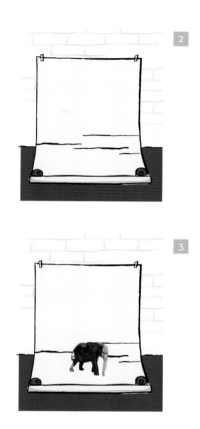

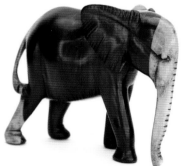

Canon EOS 50D
1/100 sec, f/4.5, ISO 200, 50mm
Heidi Adnum

Tripod

The purpose of a tripod (or monopod) is to provide stability to achieve a clearer and sharper image. It is effective in the photography of fast-moving objects but also for low-light conditions and to minimize camera shake caused by the slightest movements as the camera shutter is released. Making your own tripod can be as simple as attaching your camera to a plastic water bottle:

1. You need a plastic water bottle with lid, a metal screw that fits the tripod mount on your camera (this is often either $\frac{1}{4}$in with a $\frac{1}{20}$in thread or $\frac{3}{8}$in with a $\frac{1}{16}$in thread), a matching nut and washer, and a drill with a matching size bit. Take your camera to the hardware store if you're unsure.

2. Be careful when drilling the hole in the middle of the bottle cap.

3. Attach the screw, washer, and nut, and tighten. If you have trouble tightening the bolts, a spanner should help.

4. Fill the bottle with water. Sand can also be used as an alternative to water. Water and sand are things you don't want entering your camera, so be careful with this step and also when it comes time to use the tripod.

5. Screw the lid onto the bottle.

6. Screw the camera onto the lid.

7. Position your tripod, with camera fixed, in your photo setup.

This tripod is useful for tabletop or floor scenes and can be used as a backup to get you out of trouble. Due to its small size, it is only suitable for small, digital, compact cameras. Ultimately, however, it is a stable, raised object with a platform on which to attach or rest the camera, so alternatives can include books, shoeboxes, and fence-posts (although they are not as portable!). Owners of larger cameras should visit their local outdoors shop, as they often stock travel tripods, which are usually cheap and lightweight and very effective for everyday photography.

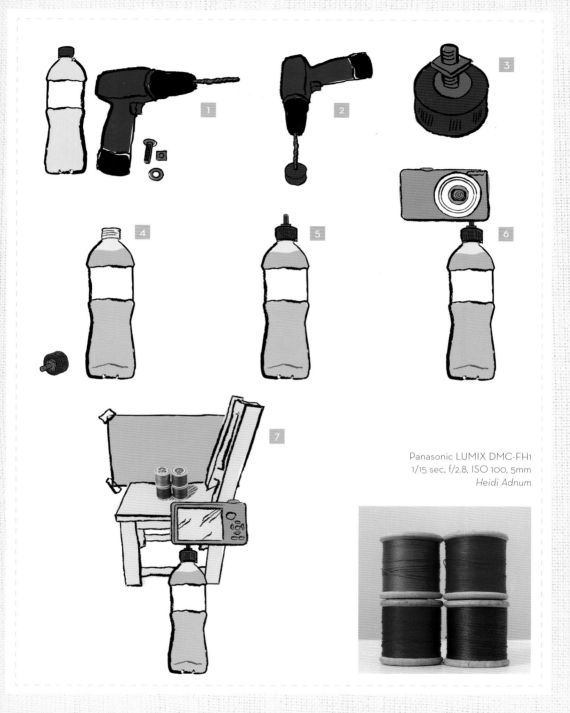

Panasonic LUMIX DMC-FH1
1/15 sec, f/2.8, ISO 100, 5mm
Heidi Adnum

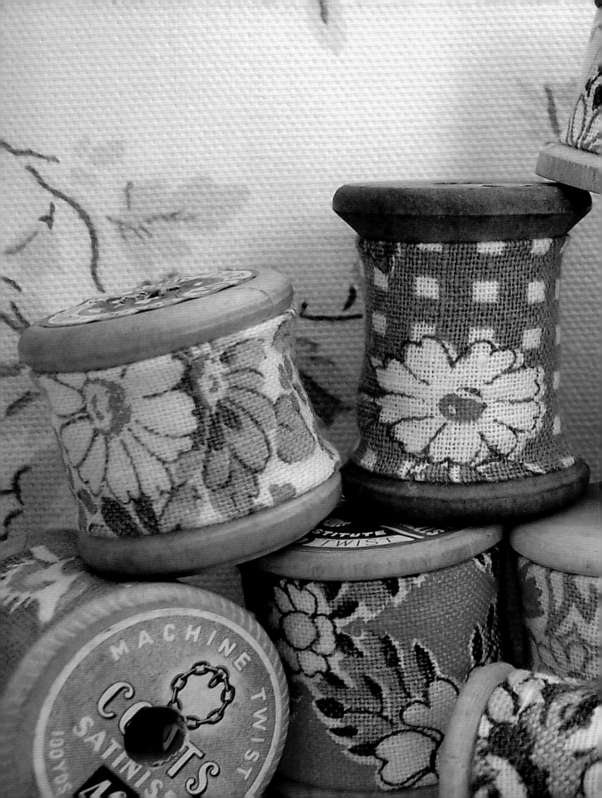

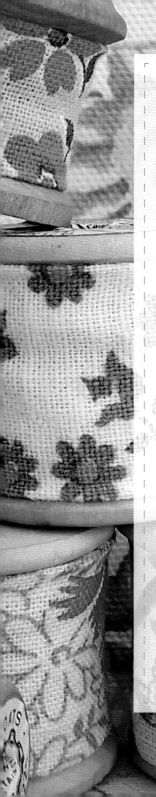

II   PHOTO FUNDAMENTALS

Planning & Setting Up

The most important thing about photographing fabrics is to make sure that you capture details like texture, color, and pattern accurately. The good news is that fashion and fabric bring a wide range of options for great photographs. Deciding on the best option for your brand will be your first step.

Suggested camera modes:
→ Portrait
→ Landscape
→ Program with low ISO
→ Shutter priority
   (especially if you're working with children)
→ Manual

Helpful equipment:
→ Tripod
→ White tile-board is helpful to have around to use as the base or platform for a mini-studio style shoot
→ A sheet of clear Plexiglas/Perspex also helps to protect and preserve paper or fabric platforms

ARTIFICIAL LIGHTING OPTION: OFF-CAMERA FLASH
Understanding and practicing with aperture, shutter, and ISO can really take your photography to the next level. With a deeper understanding of how to use light to make a great photograph, you can try off-camera flash. You can position and direct off-camera flash anywhere you like, and it can make photographing large items, such as fashions on a model or fabrics used as furniture coverings, much easier, as the light produced is so much larger and usually better quality than on-camera flash. DSLR cameras, and also many enthusiasts' compacts, are compatible with off-camera flash: look for the "hot shoe" on the top of the camera, which is the platform or mount where you attach an external flash (or the trigger)—check your camera's manual if you're unsure. If you're interested in investing in an off-camera flash, you should also consider a few other purchases to set up your own home studio. It's very easy, is accessible to everyone, and doesn't have to cost a fortune. You will need:

→ An external flash. They can be expensive, so shop around for a second-hand deal to save money. You can also look for lesser-known brands that are just as good as the major brands. It is also important to select a model that is compatible with your camera.
→ A trigger or a cable to connect the camera and the flash.
→ Batteries to power the flash and trigger.
→ A tripod or stand on which to attach the flash.

You then need to use diffusers (page 60) to soften and enlarge the light. Off-camera flash units are often used in conjunction with large, white diffusers, such as umbrellas and soft-boxes, which do exactly the same thing as the diffusers we've talked about so far: soften and enlarge the light.

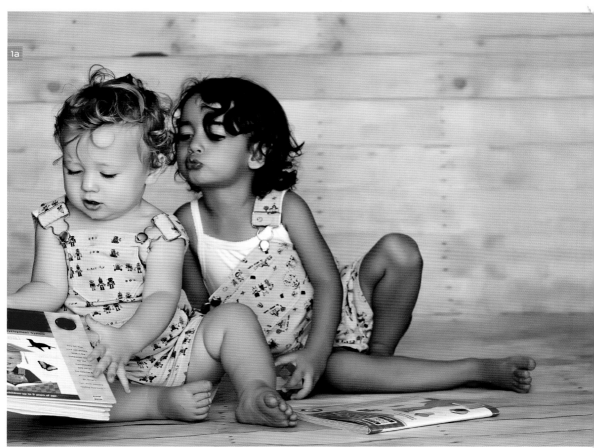

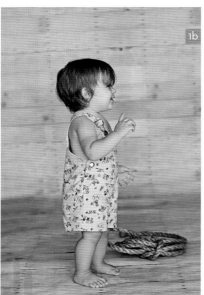

Throughout Section I we talked about the importance of soft, natural lighting, and tips and techniques for how to achieve or maximize these effects in your home or studio. In this section you should continue to think first and foremost about soft, natural lighting techniques. But we'll also consider the best ways to find and soften artificial light for those times when natural light, well, isn't coming naturally!

[1a/b] Shortalls
Canon EOS Digital Rebel XS
1/500 sec, f/2.8, ISO 400, 50mm
Emma Burcusel

Composition

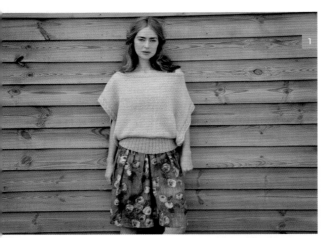

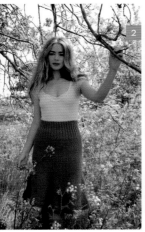

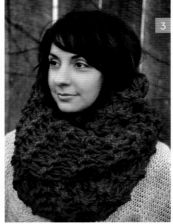

BACKGROUNDS
Neutral
Neutral backgrounds suit every product type. The neutral, seamless runway technique is one that photographers often use in the studio to shoot fashion. Learn how to create your own seamless background on page 62. If you can see the curve of the paper in your photograph and you find it distracting, it's probably because the curve is too pronounced and/or needs to fall more naturally. It can also mean your product or model is too close to the curve.

Textured
Naturally textured backgrounds, such as wooden bench-tops, are great for fabrics as they provide a subtle, earthy contrast.

In situ
An outdoors or industrial setting is another way to provide a striking contrast to fashion.

FRAMING & VIEWPOINT
For fashion, full-length shots from the front and back of the garment are a must. Your customer needs to see this to determine whether or not it will suit them and, if they can't see the details, they may move on and leave your shop for a competitor's.

If you're using models, the most flattering angles to shoot from are straight on at the same level as your model, and from just above eye-level. For another flattering angle, ask your model to stand slightly side-on with the front foot a little further forward and gently turn their torso toward you. The model can then accentuate her natural angles and curves by bending one knee and placing her hands on her hips. Photographing from slightly below eye-level can make your model seem very powerful, but too

[1] Cleo
Canon EOS 5D
1/60 sec, f/8,
ISO 100, 47mm
Vanessa Ellis

[2] Breeze
Canon EOS 5D
1/90 sec, f/4.5, ISO 100, 73mm
Vanessa Ellis

[3] Spice Oversized Tall Cowl
Nikon D700
1/80 sec, f/5.6, ISO 640, 100mm
Tori Tedesco

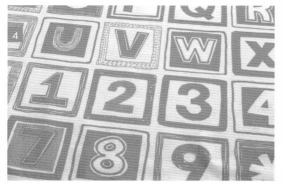
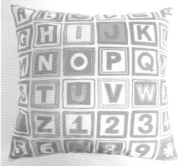
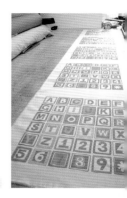

far below can be unflattering. For more interesting shots of the back of the garment, ask your model to turn her head and look over her shoulder at you, or off to the side or down.

For fabrics, shots of the full repeat are essential. Do this by laying your fabric flat and shooting from above, or, drape your fabric off the roll, out toward the camera and shoot from straight on to include the width of the entire roll and at least one repeat.

Essential for both fashion and fabric are close-up shots of the detail and texture (see page 52).

PROPS, SCALE & STYLING

In situ styling is like a serving suggestion for your customers. Models provide in situ inspiration and, as such, can be an invaluable part of your fashion photography. They help to show fit, form, shape, flow, scale, style, image, and how to wear your garments. When it comes to models, the best options are people and dressmakers' forms.

Your studio shouldn't be overlooked when you're composing your photograph, either. Offering a glimpse of the handmade process can add tremendous value to your product, giving your customer the rare opportunity to see firsthand how and where this beautiful product was made.

[4] ABC Print in Orange
Canon PowerShot G10
1/50 sec, f/4, ISO 100, 50mm
Helen Rawlinson

[5] Colorful Cubes Dog Collar
Canon EOS Digital Rebel XS
1/15 sec, f/5.6, ISO 100, 40mm
Silly Buddy

Inconsistent photographs alter the tone of your brand and shop, leaving customers and the media unsure of the direction that your brand is taking. You probably aren't exactly sure what works best for your product or where you'd like to take your brand, either. It helps to get a better idea of what photos you like—you can do that by browsing through the photographs in this book and your favorite websites and catalogs.

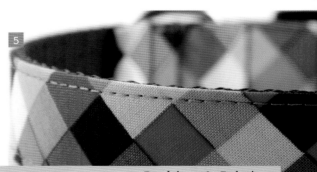

Common Problems & FAQs

Q. How do I show the scale of my fabric?

To gauge scale, we need a universal reference point, like on a map. Use the gorgeous materials and equipment involved in the manufacturing of your fabric—dressmakers' scissors, cotton spools, or paint pots are ideal. They'll also add a personal touch to your photograph. Alternatively, produce an item made from your fabric, such as a cushion, and photograph it on a chair or other standard-size piece of furniture.

Q. I get bored with using the same background, so I mix and match for variety. Is this wrong?

There are so many ways to approach photography that there is no one correct answer to this question, as it's based largely on personal opinion. Backgrounds play a crucial role in consistency, but it can be achieved in other ways such as lighting and styling. In the handmade marketplace and the mass market, you are competing with a tremendous number of other manufacturers, so you need to do everything possible to increase your chance of being seen, remembered, and making an impact. Consistency in your photographs will help you to achieve this.

Q. How can I make my fashion photographs look more professional?

Soft lighting and neutral backgrounds always look professional. Harsh shadows, under/over-exposed images, date-stamps, images that have not been rotated (turned the right way up), and revealing the edges of your background (such as the top/sides/bottom of a piece of paper taped to the wall) do not look professional.

You can employ a real model and this doesn't have to cost a fortune. You're bound to live near a model who is just getting started and looking for the experience. Place an ad in the local classifieds if you don't know where to start. Models know how to stand and pose to show off your fashions. They should be well-groomed and their stance and expression must fit with your message and image. Make the most of the model's entire outfit, using the opportunity to showcase more of your products, such as tops/bottoms and accessories.

A quality dressmaker's form (made from fabric or wood) will elicit in your customers impressions of high quality and everything being handmade. They are a superb way of showing off your fashion, especially if using a model is not viable. Vintage forms can be a very worthwhile investment and are often more beautiful than the cheap, modern versions, which can be made from plastic, foam, or metal. Search online or visit warehouse sales to pick up a form at a good price.

Mannequins are tricky. They are usually made from plastic or foam and, as a result, can look artificial. Similar to artificial flowers and vintage-look items, plastic mannequins contradict the ethos of handmade garments. You may find that they work for you, though. As a general rule, mannequins should be fully clothed for photographs, or the naked top/bottom-half cropped out of the image. If you are adding accessories, adorn your mannequin as you would a living model. For example, if you wouldn't photograph a living model with a blouse but no underwear or trousers, or if you wouldn't put an artificial flower on top of your real model's head or in front of her face, don't do it with a mannequin.

Simple but good-quality clothespins or hangers (a small version for children's fashion) also work nicely. Natural wood always implies quality, looks more professional than plastic, and won't reflect the light as much as metal. For a quality clothes hanger, shop around for a crafter who makes custom-made clothes hangers or commission a local woodworker to make one for you.

Q. How do I show the detail and texture of my fabric?

To show the detail and texture of fabric, choose one soft light source that enters the shot at an angle to your product, anywhere from zero to forty-five degrees. You can use an artificial light or off-camera flash positioned on the table near your product, or sunlight when the sun has started to set and isn't any higher than 45 degrees from the horizon. The light smoothes itself across your product and creates small shadows around a fabric's detail and texture. As the light source lifts, the shadows lessen, so, if your light source is too high, there won't be enough shadow to show fine detail. This is one of the main reasons why direct flash flattens a photograph. Combine the angle of lighting with angling your camera/lens, also up to around 45 degrees. The camera angle isn't as important as the lighting angle. But shooting from an angle can capture the effect of the light and shadows on the rows of fabric at its best. Using a camera angle such as this for your composition also helps to fill the frame with only your product, without any distractions, and this is a lovely way to show your customers the level of quality and workmanship in your product.

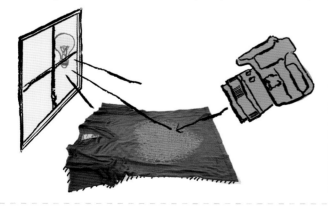

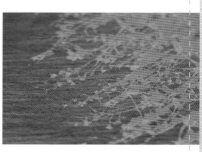

Heidi Adnum

Practitioner Spotlight
Heather Moore

How do you take photographs that show off your fabrics so beautifully?

I show the design clearly to give the viewer a sense of the texture of the basecloth and how this works with the print. I give an accurate idea of the color of the print and also impart a mood and an aesthetic within which I think my designs are situated. I take a variety of well-lit shots of the product from a number of angles, including a close-up view. I use props and furniture to show how a product could be used, and also to give the viewer a sense of what style and aesthetic my products are associated with.

Have your photographs improved since beginning your business?

They have improved. Taking my own product shots has made me very curious about how professional stylists achieve what they do. I'm in awe of their work, actually! When I've had the opportunity to attend a shoot being styled professionally, I've absorbed a lot, and then I've tried to apply what I've learned to my own shots. Watching a professional working in post-production is also hugely instructive, and I've become a lot better at photo-editing as a result. I still have so much to learn though.

Was there a point when product photography got easier for you? If so, when and why?

I bought a cheap tripod, and figured out the benefits of using a timer on a shot. Suddenly, I was able to set up the shot, set the timer, grab my reflector board, and get steady, well-lit shots without the need for any assistance.

What has been your biggest photographic challenge?

Wintertime lighting. I almost bought a light this year, but then the sun came out and didn't go away.

What do you know now that would have made photographing your fabrics and dealing with digital images easier for you in the beginning?

Planning a shot ahead, instead of just grabbing whatever is nearby, makes a great deal of difference.

What do you think are common mistakes people make when it comes to photographing fashions and fabrics?

Using overly homely settings. It's not that great to see a cushion on a sofa that looks like it has been sat on a lot.

What has been the best photography-related lesson or tip you have received?

If you have a cup in your composition, make sure there's tea in it; but if you're planning to sell the cup, don't put tea in it.

What advice do you have for other crafters who are looking for excellent photographs of their products at home or on a budget?

Find the kinds of product shots that appeal to you and study them to work out what it is about them that makes you think they are good.

Shop name
Skinny laMinx

Website
www.skinnylaminx.com

Make and model of camera
Canon PowerShot G9
and G11

Most used camera settings
Automatic

Most used camera/lighting accessories
Tripod, reflector

Favorite time of day to shoot
2pm

Favorite location
Studio

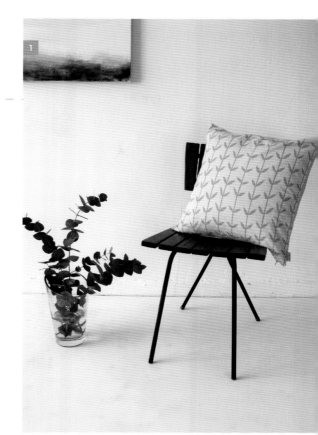

[1] Cushion made from Orla Fabric
Canon PowerShot G11
1/30 sec, f/4, ISO 80, 6.8mm

**[2] Cushions made from Sevilla
Rock Herds Fabric**
Canon PowerShot G11
1/60 sec, f/2.8, ISO 125, 7.4mm

**[3] Tea Towel made from Sevilla
Rock Herds Fabric**
Canon PowerShot G11
1/60 sec, f/2.8, ISO 100, 7.4mm

All products manufactured and
photographed by *Heather Moore*

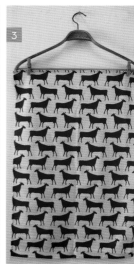

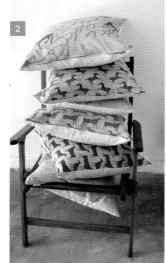

Planning & Setting Up

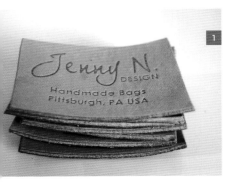

The unique details and features of handmade bags, purses, and accessories are major selling points for you and are infrequently seen in the mass-market. Show your customers how your product has been (or will be) made especially for them, and they will be impressed.

Certain items of equipment should be standard in your kit bag or shoot setup. These include spare and charged batteries, a spare memory card (or two), your camera case, neck strap, diffusers, and so on.

Suggested camera modes:
→ Macro
→ Portrait
→ Aperture priority
→ Manual

Helpful equipment:
→ Tripod
→ Reflector
→ Craft-related tools and materials

ARTIFICIAL LIGHTING OPTION: FLASHLIGHT

A flashlight/torch is a cheap and really easy-to-use source of directional light. The color and intensity of the light will depend on the type and power of the bulb, respectively. Move the flashlight closer to, or farther away from, your product for the desired effect. Choose a flashlight with a daylight/white-balanced bulb to combine with natural light. Use more than one positioned at either side of your product or just one to bring up the details. You can also use a flashlight to add light to your product from underneath or the bottom of the shot—this can make it stand out.

[1] Leather Labels
Nikon D40
1/30 sec, f/4.5, ISO 800, 32mm
Jenny Nguyen

[2] Frenchie Clutch
Canon EOS 5D MkII
1/160 sec, f/8, ISO 100, 46mm
Craig VanDerSchaegen

[3] Strappy MacBook Case
Canon EOS 5D MkII
1/8 sec, f/13, ISO 400, 46mm
J. Blake Larson

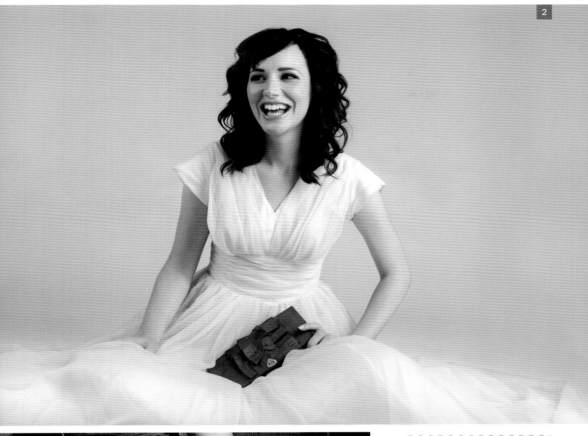

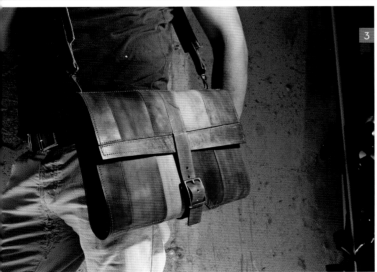

The artificial lighting tips throughout this book can work well across a range of product types. So, read through and consider how they may be applied to your area of craft.

Composition

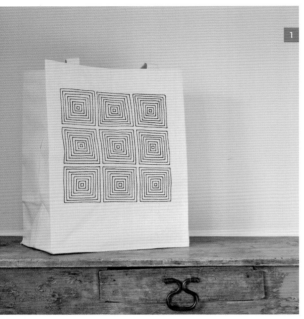

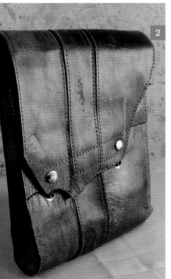

[1] Squares Tote
Nikon D90
1/50 sec, f/4.2,
ISO 250, 32mm
Pawling Print Studio

[2] NYC Hipster
Canon EOS 5D MkII
1/8 sec, f/13,
ISO 400, 46mm
J. Blake Larson

BACKGROUNDS
Neutral

There's bound to be a lot of things going on with your products, and that applies even if they are very simple in design. They're still showing off shape, color, fabric, texture, hardware, and so on. So, it's best to keep your background simple. We talked earlier about backgrounds that fall into one or more categories, and wood is one of those: It is textured and can be colored and patterned, but wood can also be beautifully neutral. Simply selecting a table, topped with an old (but clean) natural wood, positioned against a wall near a window will give you a neutral space to shoot.

Create a white seamless background if you're stuck or unsure of which background will best suit your product.

Textured

Rustic wood, brushed metal, and stone offer striking contrasts to leather. Try your hardware store for sheets of metal or mesh—the look can be earthy and industrial.

> If you have tried using wood as a background but have found the effect too strong, look for a paler, unlacquered piece. When wood is lacquered, it brings another two elements to the photograph—shine and color—and these can be overpowering, dark, and distracting.

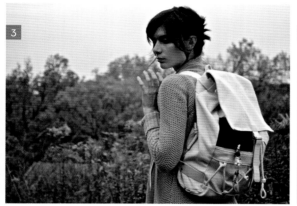

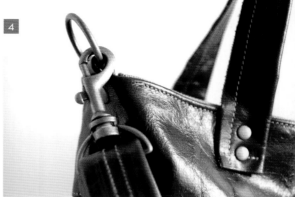

In situ

Bags, purses, and accessories are designed to go with you, so why not take them out and about for the shoot? The woods offer a perfectly coordinated color palette for natural, classic designs, and the changing seasons offer you free and updated scenes several times a year that are evocative of everything from warm and rich to light and summery feelings. Remember to shoot in the shade, or try an overcast day to avoid harsh shadows and glare.

FRAMING & VIEWPOINT

Pretending you are your customer is a sure-fire way to improve your photography: When you buy a new bag, purse, or accessory, you want to see it from the front, back, sides, and inside; you want to know how many pockets and zips it has and where they are. The best way to angle your camera is straight on. For accessories such as key rings or shoes, you can also try shooting at around a 45 degree angle to your product, allowing the product to fill the frame diagonally. Get in close or zoom in on a feature of your product.

PROPS, SCALE & STYLING

Stuff bags or purses with paper or packing materials—it will bring them to life. It is also a good idea to show the product in use so that your customer can get a feel for its true size.

Set your product down on the background or hang it from a hook or clip. Keep your props to a minimum and fill as much of the frame with your product as possible while still leaving some "breathing space" around it. This will let your product do all the talking.

[3] Wayfarer Pack
Canon EOS Digital Rebel T1i
1/50 sec, f/5.6, ISO 200, 55mm
LAYERxlayer

[4] Mini Ruche Bag
Nikon D40
1/20 sec, f/4.5, ISO 800, 32mm
Jenny Nguyen

[5] Teal Tiger Lily Moccasins
Minolta Maxxum 7000
1/100 sec, f/2.8, ISO 400, 28mm
Darlingtonia Moccasin Company

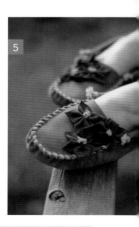

Q. How do I best show the detail in my products?
You need to use soft light and get up close to your product. Using a tripod can be very helpful to show fine detail, too. If you are finding that your bags/purses are looking a little lifeless, stuff them with crumpled paper to make them look like they are in use. This will also highlight the curves and contours of the material, allowing the light to fall on different features and soft shadows to form on others. You can also turn your product slightly to one side to show more detail.

Q. I make a wide range of purses/bags/accessories and want to inspire my customers to buy more than one. Can I do this with my photographs?
Yes. Assemble a group of your products whose colors complement each other and photograph them together. They can be positioned at different levels in the photograph, or all along in a straight line—what will look best will depend on your products. This is a great shot to have for press use.

Q. How do I make my photographs show accurately the color of my materials?
Accurate color can be achieved when the exposure and white balance are correct. Visit pages 20 and 22 to learn more. Softened natural light is the best light to choose for accurate color. Too much post-production editing can also cause inaccurate color presentation; for example, too much contrast can make colors seem darker or too saturated. See pages 146 and 148 for more information.

Q. My products are small. How do I take great photographs of them?
Use soft, balanced lighting, a tripod, your camera's self-timer and its macro setting, and get as close as you can. If you leave too much space in the photograph around your product, it can seem lost and somewhat overpowered by the sparse background. Grouping your products together can make them seem bigger and you can show off your other designs that way, too.

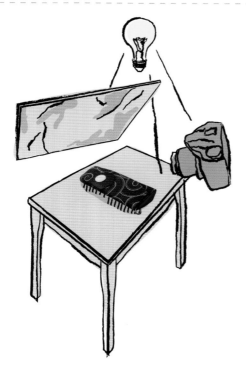

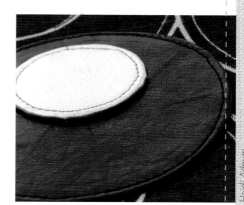

Heidi Adnum

Q. How do I show the detail and texture of leather?

Capturing the texture and detail of leather is a technique very similar to that used for fashion and fabrics, as it's a combination of a large, soft light and an angled lens. The added challenge with photographing leather is its degree of shine. Even if the leather is matte, it will still show shine at certain angles. Showing a little shine is a good thing, as it is normal and conveys depth and dimension. Showing too much shine isn't a good thing, though, as it takes the place of the detail and texture. The key to getting the balance right is to use a large, soft light. Remember that this doesn't mean finding a giant light, it means making the light source you have seem bigger by using a large white object to diffuse it, such as a shower curtain or large piece of coreflute. (Learn more about the principles of diffusing light on pages 13 and 60.) Then, position your product so that the light falls onto it at an angle. Angle your camera down onto your product until you find the position where you see mostly texture with only a little shine. See page 73 for more information.

Jenny Nguyen

How do you take photographs that show off your bags so beautifully?

Because selling online does not allow for the touch sensation, I try to capture the feel of the bag in each image, showing all the subtle details of each piece as if someone were looking at it in person. I keep the background simple and photograph in natural light. I like to show the grains of the leather, stitching, color, pleats, and folds to show the drape of the material. Keep it simple!

Has your photographic process changed the way you make your bags?

Yes, greatly. Originally I used props to showcase my products, but I felt that it was diverting attention away from the actual product. That is when I realized that I may have been using props as a crutch to hide any flaws in my design. I improved my designs over time and no longer needed props to improve the look of my photography. The product itself is the showcase item.

Have your photographs improved since beginning your business? If so, how?

My photographs have improved greatly since the beginning of my business. I started with using white foam board on the bottom and back of my images, hung my bags on a thumbtack and took each photograph with the camera flash. I then upgraded to a fabric backdrop and floodlights. With those methods, I spent hours correcting the color and background of the images. Now, I have a simple, white table set against a white wall placed in an area of my studio that receives great natural sunlight. I process the images very little before they get published. I spend maybe five minutes at

most on each product photograph, just resizing the image to work on the website and correcting items such as brightness of the image.

Was there a point when product photography got easier for you? If so, when and why?

Product photography got easier for me after I started photographing my products in natural light. I use an inexpensive DSLR. Before that, I used an inexpensive point-and-shoot, but the photographs from that camera and my new camera are still quite similar.

What has been your biggest photographic challenge?

The biggest photographic challenge is when I have new products to photograph and the weather is stormy and dark for many days. My easy fix is using my tripod and increasing the exposure of the image. It usually turns out just fine!

What do you know now that would have made photographing your bags and dealing with digital images easier for you in the beginning?

I wish I knew that photographing with natural light is always better than artificial light. No artificial light is brighter than sunlight. It has made a world of difference in the ease of photographing and also processing after a photo shoot. I would recommend this to all crafters.

What do you think are common mistakes people make when it comes to photographing bags, purses, and accessories?

Using an undiffused flash, choosing a busy background, and poor composition.

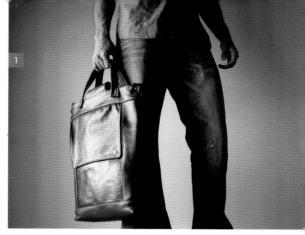

Shop name
Jenny N. Design

Website
www.jennyndesign.com

Make and model of camera
Formerly a Sony DSC-H5 and now
Nikon D40

Most used camera settings
Automatic with timer and
manual-focus lens

Most used camera/ lighting accessories
Tripod

Favorite time of day to shoot
Early morning and late afternoon

Favorite location
On a table next to a window that
receives ample sunlight

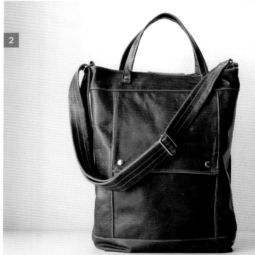

[1] Briefcase
Sony DSC-H5
1/40 sec, f/2.8, ISO 200, 6.6mm

[2] Briefcase
Nikon D40
1/15 sec, f/4.2, ISO 800, 28mm

[3] Mini Ruche Bag
Nikon D40
1/15 sec, f/3.5, ISO 800, 19mm

All products manufactured and
photographed by *Jenny Nguyen*

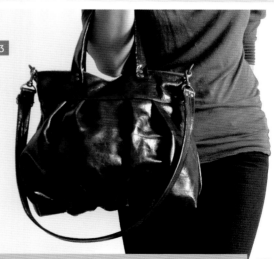

Planning & Setting Up

Your photographs need to give your customers a sense of how your product feels, just by looking at it. Do this by using soft lighting and including close-up shots of the intricate and delicate features of your products.

Suggested camera modes:
→ Macro
→ Aperture priority
→ Manual

Helpful equipment:
→ Tripod
→ Reflector
→ Tools such as knitting/crochet needles

There are two attributes that are important with any light— the hardness/softness and the power of the light. They are both related as they both change over distance; for example, a light of a fixed size and power will appear more powerful and soft when close to the subject, compared to the same light when further away from the subject (which is less powerful and harder).

ARTIFICIAL LIGHTING OPTION: LED BOOK LIGHTS

LED book lights are small, lightweight and cheap, directional, and can be clipped on to a surface for extra stability. They are usually white, so won't cause a color-cast and can be combined with daylight. Their small heads make them suitable for use with more delicate crafts, such as knitting, crochet, needlecraft, and felting; but don't be fooled by their small size—such a light can still be pretty powerful at close range. To reduce the power, move the light further away from your craft. If moving the light away makes the shadows worse, bigger, and darker (i.e., makes the light harder), keep them close to your craft and diffuse the light by covering the head with semi-opaque white plastic. Fashion this out of a white, empty, clean, and dry milk container or cosmetic bottle.

[1] Kid's Aviator Hat
Canon EOS 5D MkII
1/200 sec, f/4.5, ISO 200, 85mm
Olga Courtnage

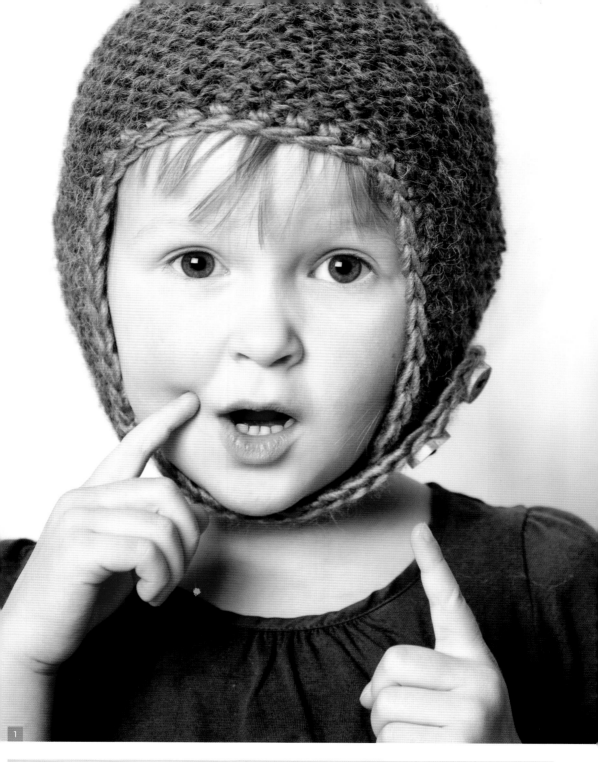

Composition

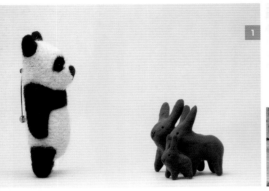

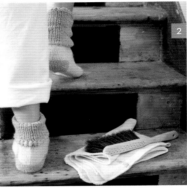

[1] Felted Panda Brooch
Canon EOS
Digital Rebel XSi
1/100 sec, f/13,
ISO 100, 100mm
Emīlija Lielā

[2] Handknit Bedsocks
Bronica
1/15 sec, f/5.6,
ISO 100, 150mm
Lucy Pope

BACKGROUNDS
Neutral
Yet again, neutral backgrounds are ideal platforms for the delicate and intricate features of knitting and needlecraft.

Some natural backgrounds can seem like a good idea for a neutral background (e.g., pebbles, rocks, and grass), but even though they are naturally beautiful scenes/objects, they are usually high contrast and full of detail, such as shapes and colors, so they can be distracting. They are normally positioned in hard light (direct sunlight) so, at the very least, require a diffuser to soften their appearance. Also, a photograph showing a product placed on a platform looks more thoughtful than one placed directly on the ground.

Textured
Use fabric as your background. Select colors that are neutral or complementary, and even layer them up for a rich, sumptuous feel.

In situ
Show your products where they are intended to be used, whether out on the street or in the home. This can convey a sense of coziness and warmth.

If you're finding that in situ shots are too cluttered and take too much attention and focus away from your product, simplify by removing everything from the scene and then repositioning them, one by one. You'll see just how many things are in your scene and you'll start to reject the things that really aren't important.

FRAMING & VIEWPOINT

The textures of wool, felt, and other materials used in knitting and needlework are seductive. Their softness is associated with comfort and pleasure. You can capitalize on this by getting up close and filling the frame with your product. Try a 45-degree angle or shoot from directly above.

When you're framing the shot, take one photograph and look at it before continuing. Reposition the camera to avoid distractions or other meaningless information. Cropping by moving the camera closer and/or zooming in on your product will save you time later on in post-production.

Framing your photograph with your point-of-interest to one side can be interesting and quirky. The same effect can be achieved by framing to exclude typical features of a photograph; for example, showing most but not all of a face is perfectly acceptable and can be very creative.

PROPS, SCALE & STYLING

Above all, keep it simple. Vintage toys, if they are appropriate for your product type, send messages of quality, of being handmade, of history, and of playfulness. Beautiful home décor and settings are ideal to inspire your customers.

Continue to look to your studio or workplace for inspiration. Balls of wool, spools of thread, piles of felt, buttons, beads, and scissors make lovely, thoughtful props.

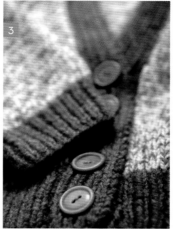
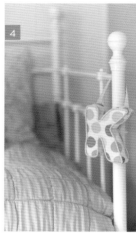
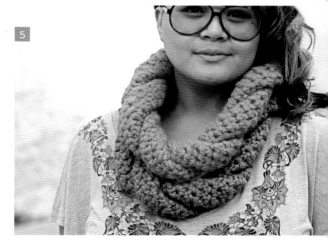

[3] Pick and Mix Baby Cardigan
Nikon D2X S11
1/125 sec, f/2.8, ISO 400, 78mm
Phil Wilkinson

[4] Little Love Letter
Canon EOS 1D MkII
1/100 sec, f/2, ISO 50, 100mm
Bill Bradshaw

[5] Hollis Rope Chain
Nikon D80
1/60 sec, f/4, ISO 200, 50mm
Hurley Sashimi

Common Problems & FAQs

Q. What is the best background for knitting and needlecraft?
The best background is subtle, gentle, and complementary. Avoid very dark backgrounds (e.g., pure black or white), as they're too harsh. You want the focus of the image to be on your beautiful product and not props and elaborate styling.

Q. The light in my house always changes and I can't achieve consistently good photographs. What should I do?
First of all, you should group your shoots into batches, if possible, and shoot quite a few pieces on one day when the light is available. When this isn't possible, go outside. In the depths of winter, go outside in the middle of the day. This is something that we're normally warned against for good photography, as the light is too harsh, but give it a try if you're really struggling. Use a diffuser to soften the shadows if it's still too harsh. Snowy scenes can be light and dreamy. If you need to stay inside, find a time when the light through the biggest window in your home is most abundant and shoot at that time every day. Add in a reflector to maximize the effect. See pages 58 and 59 for more.

Q. My products are so soft and floppy that I find them hard to style. What can I do?
It's very frustrating when one of the best features of your product is also the reason why it's difficult to photograph! You can use a soft filler, like wool or cotton, for products with an "inner." Pile up a selection of your products, as this will give them more structure and depth, and it will also help to fill the frame of the photograph. For those that don't suit piling up, hang them together, or use a model or dressmakers' form.

Q. My knitwear is contemporary and my target market is both men and women. How do I style contemporary, unisex photographs?
If we said that the masculine/feminine scale of photographs starts with feminine on the left, neutral in the middle, and masculine at the right, you want to aim to style your photograph somewhere around the middle, possibly with a swing to the right. You can't go wrong with neutral minimalist. Achieve this by using a neutral background and few or no props. Urban chic will also appeal to both men and women. Use street scenes and weathered building signs. Residential scenes, such as brick walls and industrial settings like cement walls, steps, and other building materials, can also look interesting, minimalist, and unisex. Choose an overcast or cloudy day for less harsh shadows and add in fill light, if necessary (see page 15).

Q. When I photograph my knitting close up to show its finest detail, the photographs turn out blurry. Help!

Knitting and needlecraft offer some of the finest detail and most beautiful and sumptuous textures in the handmade marketplace. In order to capture the detail and texture of these products, it is essential to keep the camera very still. A tripod will be helpful, but sometimes it's not possible or convenient to use a tripod. It's at such times that stabilizing yourself against a nearby sturdy object can help to improve your photography by achieving sharp focus. Rest on a wall, table, or bring in another sturdy object and place it near your scene.

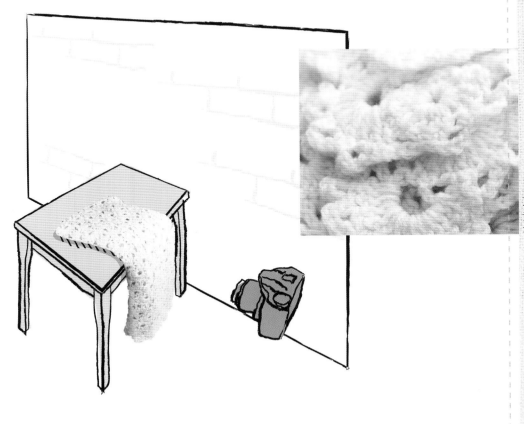

Heidi Adnum

Practitioner Spotlight
Jenny Gordy

How do you take photographs that show off your knitting and needlecraft so beautifully?

I prefer natural, soft lighting and try to take my photographs in indirect sunlight whenever possible. I never use flash and I try to avoid incandescent and fluorescent lighting. A 50mm lens allows for a wonderfully shallow depth of field, which blurs the background nicely.

How do you show accurate color, along with detail and texture, in your photographs?

I try to set my white balance appropriately and fiddle around with it while shooting to get the right colors. For the times that it doesn't work out, I change the color in post-production.

Can you tell us if there was a point at which product photography became easier for you? If so, when and why?

When I bought my DSLR camera and lens, it was a dream come true. Since then, studying photographs I love has helped me figure out my style. Emulating others I admire has brought me a long way.

What do you think are common mistakes people make when it comes to photographing knitting and needlecraft?

Lack of detail, poor lighting, cluttered background, ugly dressmakers' form, or creepy mannequin head.

Can you share any advice for other crafters who are looking to take excellent product photographs at home or on a budget?

Whatever camera you have, consider every detail when photographing your product. A clean background is essential, even if you have to move around some furniture. Photographs should have a nice range of tones, and you should be able to see detail in the shadows as well as the highlights. Shooting in good, natural light and learning how to use your camera's settings will help with this, as can time in post-production. Remember that with a photograph that's too light, you lose information, so it's best to take a photograph that's a little too dark and possibly lighten it later in post-production. Play around with the white-balance setting on your camera. And don't forget to practice! Sometimes you'll take a hundred bad photographs, but the one good one will be worth it.

What do you know now that would have made photographing your knitting and needlecraft and dealing with digital images easier for you in the beginning?

Natural-looking photographs are always better than excessively vivid colors or overly contrasting tones. Also, I learned when my computer crashed that I should have been backing up my files. Now I save all my digital images to an external hard drive.

What has been the best photography-related lesson or tip you have received?

My photography professor in college constantly told me to practice the different settings on my camera and actually read the instruction manual so that I knew what everything was. I'm still practicing by trying new things, and I'm always forcing myself to learn more instead of relying on the automatic settings. The more I practice and the more research I do, the better my photographs turn out.

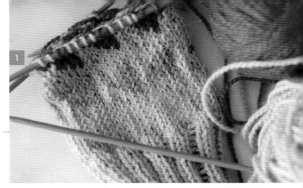

Shop name
Wiksten

Website
www.wikstenmade.com

Make and model of camera
Nikon D80

Most used camera settings
Manual

Most used camera/lighting accessories
Tripod and wireless remote control

Favorite time of day to shoot
Morning

Favorite location
In a beautiful home with lots of light

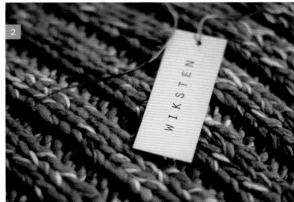

[1] Triangle Socks
Nikon D80
1/30 sec, f/2.8, ISO 640, 50mm

[2] Marled Loop Scarf
Nikon D80
1/80 sec, f/1.4, ISO 640, 50mm

[3] Handknit Socks
Nikon D80
1/60 sec, f/5.3, ISO 640, 40mm

All products manufactured and photographed by *Jenny Gordy*

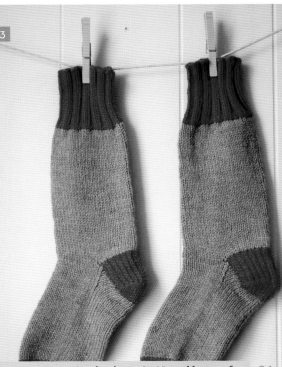

Planning & Setting Up

Your challenge is to ensure that your customers can make the very personal decision to purchase an item of jewelry to wear based solely upon your photographs. Creating photographs that show off the custom-made detail, shine, scale, and wearability of your work will help your customers connect to your work.

Suggested camera modes:
→ Macro
→ Aperture priority
→ Manual

Helpful equipment:
→ Tripod
→ Macro lens
→ Remote control
→ Reflector, white and black
→ Daylight-balanced travel lights or book lights

ARTIFICIAL LIGHTING OPTION: TRAVEL LIGHTS

Use a set of battery-operated, white-bulb, gooseneck travel lights to light the back of your scene (backlighting). Position the travel light behind your jewelry so that the light softly drifts over your background and product. Diffuse the light with white fabric (keep an eye on it in case it gets too hot) or use smaller book lights if the light is too strong.

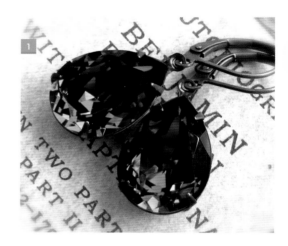

[1] Estate Earrings
Canon PowerShot SX20 IS
1/160 sec, f/2.8, ISO 80, 5mm
Lara Lewis

[2] Fever Teardrop Necklace
Nikon Coolpix L100
1/265 sec, f/4.3, ISO 80, 12.2mm
Celia Boaz

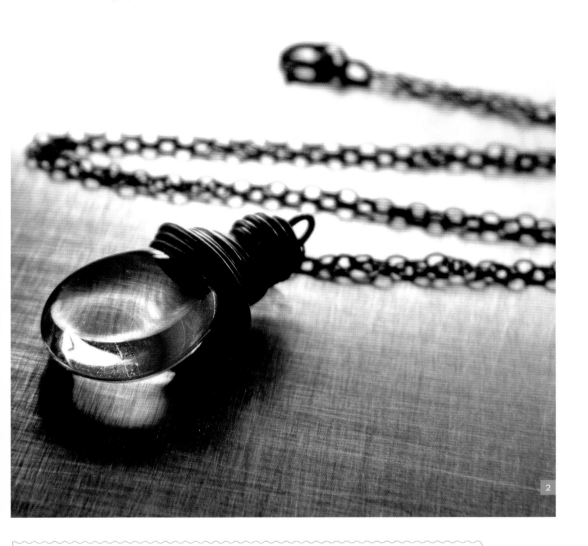

2

Remember that any light source, whether physically big or small, can be a hard light. The sun is the best example of this concept. The sun is unimaginably large, but when it is blazing down on us from so far away, undiffused at full power, it is a very hard and small light, causing harsh shadows, glare, and lost detail. When the sun is diffused with clouds, trees, or sheer-white fabric, for example, it becomes more spread out and, therefore, a larger, softer light.

Composition

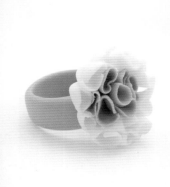

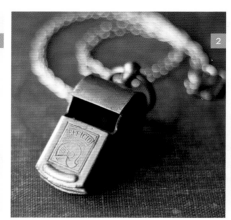

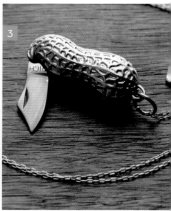

[1] Aragonesa Purple Porcelain Ring
Olympus E-500
1/200 sec, f/3.5, ISO 100, 45mm
MaaPstudio

**[2] Contrary Antique Efficio
Whistle Necklace**
Canon EOS Digital Rebel XSi
1/100 sec, f/3, ISO 100, 50mm
Mary Andrews

[3] Contrary Peanut Knife Necklace
Canon EOS Digital Rebel XSi
1/100 sec, f/3, ISO 100, 50mm
Mary Andrews

BACKGROUNDS
Neutral

Darker, neutral backgrounds will help your jewelry
to stand out, especially if they are light in color or
metallic. It is essential to use soft lighting, preferably
from behind or to the side, to show the texture of
your product and the background.

If your jewelry is intricate and you find it difficult to
light, try a light tent (page 54) or a light box (page 56)
to provide soft wraparound light.

Textured

Whether your product is rustic, edgy, or refined,
it will look great on a textured background.
Try the subtle and understated texture and
colors of vintage book covers, natural woods,
and matte leather.

The contrast between a shiny, polished metal and
natural wood is sublime and adds a certain depth
to the photograph.

Fabric is also going to complement your product. Use the back of a chair or a book cover or a covered cork board. Select a shade that is complementary to your product, e.g., gray linen with silver/metal.

It's not just the outside of vintage books that work wonderfully. Open them up to reveal beautifully colored and textured pages.

FRAMING AND VIEWPOINT

Your customers won't be able to look away if you fill almost the entire frame with your product. Shooting from above your product allows you to fill the frame with your background, too, so you don't have to worry about showing the edge of the table or the wall behind your scene. Allow your product to float in from the top or the right/left/top side of the photograph for a gentle, fluid feel. Don't be afraid to compose to show only one main feature of your product for the headline shot. Leaving out details can be powerful, too. It implies that everything you need to tell your story with this product is right there.

PROPS, SCALE & STYLING

Look to your packaging for inspiration: beautiful jewelry boxes can be the perfect prop, and vintage dress forms make gorgeous props and also show scale and a thoughtful style.

The small, intricate nature of most jewelry means that it doesn't take much to overpower it in a photograph. If you shed the excess information in your scene and stick to your background and product alone, you'll take a better photograph. This can apply also to props, so leave them out if you're unsure.

[4] Violaine Necklace
Nikon D3000
1/30 sec, f/3.5, ISO 320, 18mm
Lisa Bruemmer

**[5] Faceted Gold Vermeil
Nugget Necklace**
Canon PowerShot SD1000
1/60 sec, f/2.8, ISO 200, 5.8mm
Julie Garland

[6] Theresa Necklace
Nikon D3000
1/15 sec, f/4.2, ISO 400, 26mm
Lisa Bruemmer

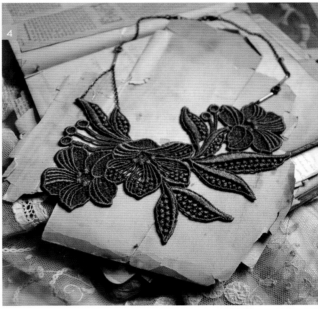

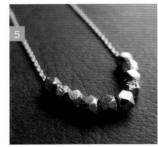

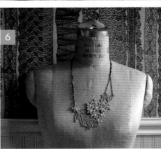

Common Problems & FAQs

Q. I want to photograph my jewelry on a reflective surface and I used a mirror, but it doesn't look right. What else can I try?

Shiny surfaces will add a liquid-like extension to your product and this can look luxurious, so it's an excellent idea. The problem with using a mirror is that the reflection has effectively doubled the amount of information in your photograph and, therefore, is crowding the shot and distracting your customer. The key is to use a reflective surface that won't provide an exact image of your product, but will offer a softened, subtle reflection, like a gentle, colored shadow. Use a household tile or enameled wood for a soft reflection. You can also try a sheet of clear acrylic, glass, or Perspex laid over the top of card.

Q. How do I show translucence of gemstones in photographs?

You should consider angle and lighting. When styling your photograph, you may need to tilt your product slightly up or down or to the side to best show its features, or it may look best from directly above; each stone will be different. If soft, natural light isn't that easy to find, experiment with a light box (page 56). If lit softly from the side or from behind, the light will fall onto the gemstone and bounce around inside it. If lit from straight on, the light bounces off the gemstone, often reflecting back up to the camera lens, so all you see is the surface of the gemstone. If you use hard light, such as undiffused on-camera flash, all your camera will see is the harsh reflection on the gemstone, not the light coming through.

Q. How do I avoid reflection when photographing shiny jewelry?

Reflection may seem like a bad thing but, like shadows, some reflection is important. The right amount of reflection adds depth to inanimate objects and makes them look more realistic. Metal and other shiny surfaces will reflect all the things around them. Any shiny/reflective surface that is positioned straight at the camera will also reflect the lens/lighting/photographer; this is difficult to avoid without digital editing. When you consider all of these things, trying to eliminate all reflection amounts to trying to create an unnatural image of your product and, in many ways, is a waste of time.

There are, however, ways to reduce the amount of reflection if it is bothering you. Zoom in so that the camera/lens is further away from your jewelry and/or use the timer so you can walk out of range of the shot. Rest assured, though, that if your customers are looking at a sharp, detailed, and well-lit photograph, a reflection in the product would not be a problem.

Q. Some of my customers have commented that they thought my earrings were smaller/bigger than they really are. How do I photograph jewelry to show its size?

The easiest way to show the size of your jewelry is to photograph it on a model. You don't have to use a scale photograph as your headline image, just include it in the additional photographs.

Q. When I photograph sterling silver jewelry, it looks white and too bright, even though the exposure is ideal. I've turned the flash off and I'm using diffused natural light. What am I doing wrong?

When photographing jewelry, especially pieces that are smooth and bright, you need to use soft-light without on-camera flash. If the metal, such as silver, looks too dark and flat, the image is probably underexposed. If it is otherwise well-lit but still looks flat and rather boring, this is probably because there isn't enough contrast between the lighter and darker areas on the metal to show its natural shine and dimension. This contrast is caused by reflected light and you can add in a dark reflector to add contrast and enhance the contours of the jewelry. Use a piece of black card and position it near to the metal until you can see the dark reflection. You will notice that the closer you position the black card, the stronger the reflection. This technique works really well when the setting is well-lit and the metal is highly reflective. You can also combine black card with white card for a more controlled effect.

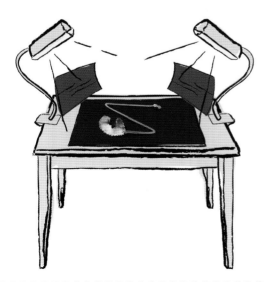

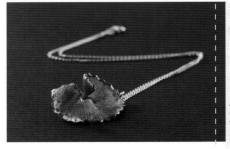

Heidi Adnum

Practitioner Spotlight
Michelle Chang

How do you take photographs that show off your work so beautifully?
I show each piece of my jewelry clearly. I use natural indirect/diffused lighting by shooting next to a window inside my home during daylight hours and use a good-quality camera.

Has your photographic process changed the way you make your jewelry?
Yes. I know that my camera picks up the tiniest detail and flaw, so I make my jewelry sample piece with care and precision to avoid spending time in post-production cleaning up my mistakes.

Have your photographs improved since beginning your business? If so, how?
The way I take photographs has definitely evolved. I started with a white light tent, placed my jewelry in the box, and used mini photographic lighting on stands. Now I only use natural lighting and place my jewelry on a neutral, dark-gray stone tile.

How do you show the detail of your jewelry?
I shoot with the focal point on the area of the piece that I want highlighted. Often, I shoot a few different angles of the same piece—one might be a close-up and another pulled back for a full view.

When did photographing your crafts get easier?
When I decided to use natural lighting. I realized that often, if the lighting is optimal, I could shoot with automatic setting and focus with great results, just as good as if I shoot manually. This happened after about six months of shooting. Also, with natural light and a simple setup, the setup time is pretty short, as I didn't have to use any props, light boxes, setup lights, and so on.

What do you know now that would have made photographing your jewelry and processing digital images easier for you in the beginning?
I was a real novice with the camera before I started my jewelry line and I was not very familiar with editing software. I now have a routine for setting up my pieces to get the best angles for the different types of jewelry I make. Also, I'm much more adept at using Adobe Photoshop for my needs.

What do you think are common mistakes people make when it comes to photographing jewelry?
I think people often don't realize that detail shots are necessary, especially when a piece is three-dimensional, as is the case with some of my jewelry. Also, that good cropping and composition can make all the difference.

What has been the best photography-related lesson or tip you have received?
Consistency is very important. You want to have your online shop look as cohesive as possible.

What advice do you have for other crafters who are looking for excellent photographs of their products at home or on a budget?
Get a good camera to start. Get a good macro lens for details and close-ups, especially if your product is small and showing detail is important. Get very familiar with software that you use to touch up and finalize your photographs. Be consistent with your product shots by deciding the optimal setup for your product, i.e., natural light, type of backdrop, etc.

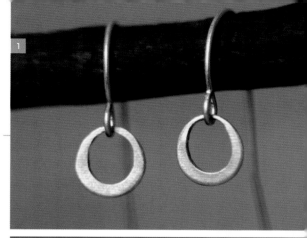

Shop name
Michelle Chang Jewelry

Website
www.michellechang.com

Camera
Canon EOS 30D

Most used camera settings
1/60 sec, f/2.8, 100mm

Most used camera/lighting accessories
Tripod, remote shutter release

Favorite time of day to shoot
Mid to late afternoon

Favorite location
Indoors, next to a window

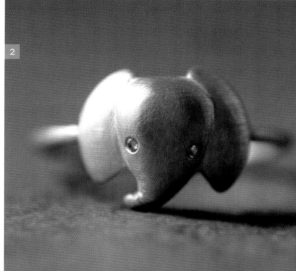

[1] Gold hoop earrings
Canon EOS 30D
1/60 sec, f/2.8, ISO 400, 100mm

[2] Elephant ring
Canon EOS 30D
1/60 sec, f/2.8, ISO 400, 100mm

[3] Heart necklace
Canon EOS 30D
1/60 sec, f/2.8, ISO 400, 100mm

All products manufactured and
photographed by *Michelle Chang*

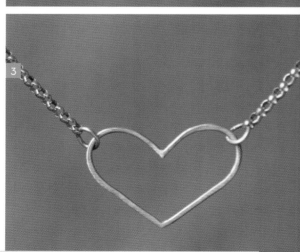

Jewelry

Planning & Setting Up

Dolls and toys evoke powerful thoughts, feelings, and memories for us, as they are directly linked to the past and to special times in our childhood. Fill your photographs with feeling and character by selecting the right background, composition, and framing.

Suggested camera modes:
→ Landscape
→ Macro
→ Sport (if you're working with children)
→ Aperture priority
→ Shutter priority (also if you're working with children)
→ Manual

Helpful equipment:
→ Tripod
→ Flash diffuser
→ Colored backgrounds

ARTIFICIAL LIGHTING OPTION: ON-CAMERA FLASH

On-camera flash is a small light that produces a quick burst of undiffused light at close range, and so is a hard light. You can use on-camera flash as a soft(er) light, though, by diffusing the flash (page 60) and using the fill-light technique (page 15). If you use diffused on-camera flash with a semi-automatic or manual setting in combination with natural light, you can achieve a very nice result. We've talked about attaching cut-to-size white paper and semi-opaque white plastic to the camera; other suggestions for flash diffusers include white foam and thick, white fabric.

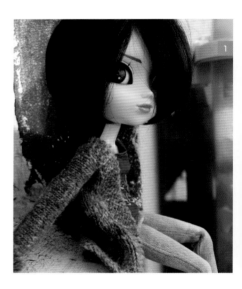

If you do need to use artificial light in your product photography, remember to use only one type of light to avoid color-cast (read more on pages 22 and 55).

**[1] Knitted Cardigan for Pullip
and Momoko Dolls**
Panasonic DMC-FZ250
1/320 sec, f/3.2, ISO 200, 8.7mm
Blanca González

**[2] Hoodie and Leggings
for PukiPukis**
Nikon D80
1/1.3 sec, f/13, ISO 400, 48mm
Helle Gavin

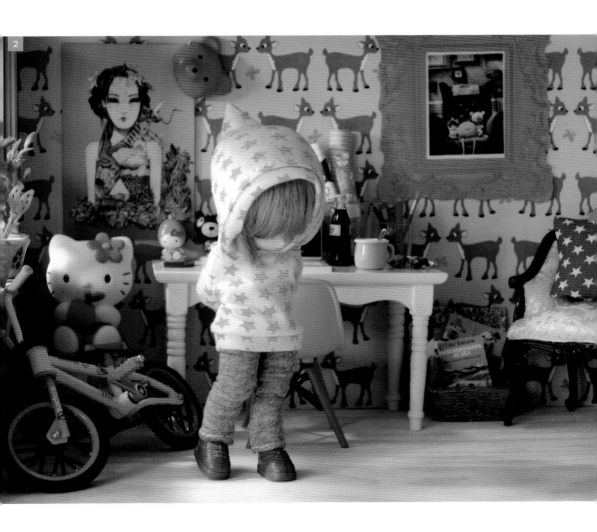

Composition

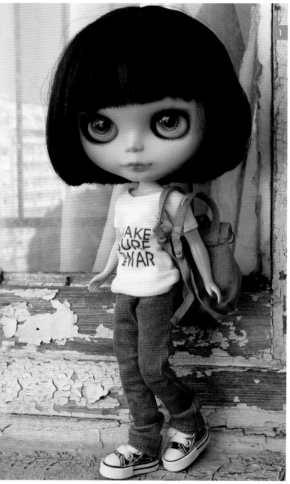

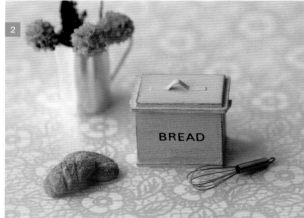

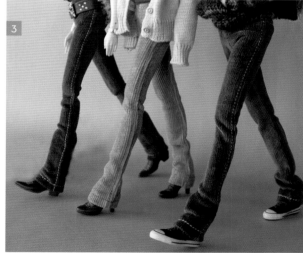

[1] Make Surf Not War for Blythe Doll
Panasonic DMC-FZ250
1/250 sec, f/3.2, ISO 200, 9.6mm
Blanca González

[2] Dollhouse Miniature Bread Box
Canon EOS Digital Rebel XSi
1/60 sec, f/4, ISO 100, 100mm
Pei Li Chin

[3] Cords for Pullip and Momoko Dolls
Panasonic DMC-FZ250
1/60 sec, f/3.2, ISO 100, 14.8mm
Blanca González

[4] Wand, Crown, and Cape Set
Nikon D300
1/100 sec, f/5.6, ISO 320, 35mm
Erin Riley

BACKGROUNDS

Neutral

If your toys are speaking to the girls' and boys' market, go for a neutral background. You won't alienate any customers or box yourself in to either gender.

Textured

Cardstock is a great way to include understated texture in your background. You can also look around your home or neighborhood for other interesting scenes.

Color

Have fun with colored backgrounds. They create a layered effect and are often used in merchandising to attract attention. It's very important to select colors that will enhance the color in your product. The best guide is to use a complementary color in the same shade as your craft.

Patterned

Stripes, dots, or subtle florals are great options for dolls and toys. Try wallpaper, gift wrap, and fabric for different designs.

FRAMING & VIEWPOINT

Dolls and toys afford you quite a bit of flexibility when it comes to the orientation and framing of your product. Make eye-contact with your customer by shooting straight on. Shoot from slightly below to exaggerate a particular feature, such as shoes or wheels.

Crop out information to focus in on a particular feature or detail.

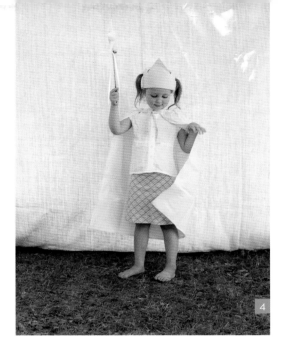

PROPS, SCALE & STYLING

Makers of dolls and toys have the green light to be playful and have fun with their photographs. When you shoot in a neat, clean, and clear environment, your customers will know that you have put a lot of thought and care into the photograph, and they will then assume the same of your work.

Including a child as a model is a great idea for photographing dolls and toys. You'll struggle to find a cuter prop or way of showing scale than that!

When using contrasting colors, such as warms and cools, approach with care: this can change the mood of your photograph and be uncomfortable to look at.

Common Problems & FAQs

Q. How can I show humor/fun in my photographs?
Let your product do the talking by keeping the setting simple. You may decide on a neutral background or a more textured, colorful, garden setting, but keep the props and other styling to a minimum. Position your product off-center and show all of its features, whether it's long limbs, a flouncy tail, or huge ears, as that conveys a sense that the photograph is a portrait, and a special portrait of a doll/toy is bound to make your customers smile. Also, taking your dolls/toys outside and to unusual places can make it seem like they're on an adventure.

Q. My children are my models, but my photographs are always blurry and the camera won't take the photograph fast enough. What can I do?
To create in-focus photographs of moving objects, you need to use a fast shutter speed and keep the camera very still. Hold the camera with both hands and try using the sport mode or shutter priority on your camera. Photographing children makes using a tripod rather difficult; as soon as you've got it set up, they're gone! A monopod is more practical, if you'd like more stability. Set your camera to continuous mode, which instructs the camera to open and close the shutter several times at once, while you have the shutter-release pressed down.

Q. My compact camera doesn't have shutter priority or continuous mode. Is there anything else I can do?
Digital compact cameras can suffer from lag between the time that the shutter button is pressed and the time that the camera actually takes the photograph. Sport mode is probably your best solution, other than upgrading to a DSLR. Faster shooting or less lag time is one of the features you are paying for when you invest in a DSLR.

Q. My apartment is small and mostly dark with no space for photo shoots. What can I do?
Pick the best space in your apartment that is near a window and prune everything back. Move tables and chairs and other clutter until you've got a completely blank canvas of floor and wall, and remove the curtains as well. You may then need to clean the wall and skirting boards a little, so that no marks show up in the photograph. Depending on the look you're going for, return the objects that you need, such as a table and one potted plant. You're almost guaranteed a better photograph if there is less in it to distract the eye. To increase the available light, you can try the tips below, or, you could invest in some small book/travel lights (page 92). If the color of your walls

is bugging you, try creating your own white or colored background—learn how to make one on pages 62 and 129. If you absolutely can't find a large enough clear space to shoot, make a light tent (page 54) and position it near a window.

Q. Window light isn't enough to light my toys in my home/studio. Is there anything I can do?
Sometimes using one method of increasing available light just isn't enough. However, if you use a combination of the techniques we've talked about so far, you will find that it is a great way to maximize light and combat low-light conditions. Use window light (page 12) as well as a reflector (page 58) and diffused flash (page 60) to dramatically increase the amount of light that falls onto your product. Remember that you can redirect the flash to the ceiling with white card (shown here), that is, if covering the flash with paper doesn't offer enough diffusion. The soft effect gained from these techniques is perfect for delicately textured and colored dolls and toys.

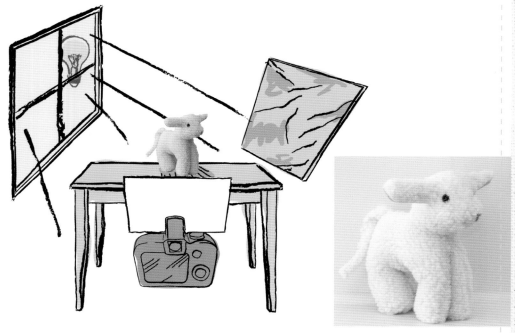

Heidi Adnum

Practitioner Spotlight
Erin Freuchtel-Dearing

How do you take photographs that show off your toys so beautifully?

I think I can truly attribute my photographs to patience and attention to detail. You might get lucky and take a few good shots once in a while, but if you approach your photography almost as if it were a science, you will more than likely get consistently high-quality photos. Find out what formula of background, lighting, and angles shows off your product best and then work on refining your photos. Don't be afraid of re-photographing a product to see if you can get even better photos.

How do you show accurate color, along with detail and texture, in your photographs?

I believe that using indirect/diffused natural light is the easiest way to get true color. If the color looks a bit off in the photos, I will occasionally do a bit of color correction in post-production.

What has been your biggest photographic challenge?

I would have to say that lighting is my biggest struggle. Since I use natural light exclusively, it can be difficult to find the perfect light to shoot in. It took a while to find the right place during the right time of day in my home, since there is not a great deal of natural light.

Can you tell us if there was a point when product photography got easier for you?

I took tons of photographs over the first few months, with many types of lighting, with different backgrounds and camera settings. After reviewing all of them, I chose the background and lighting that consistently showed my work off well. It really

was trial and error and time taken getting to know my camera that helped me to become comfortable with taking photographs of our toys.

What do you think are common mistakes when it comes to photographing dolls and toys?

I think one of the biggest mistakes is that people don't take enough photos from a variety of different angles. Most often the potential customer will not be able to see or touch your product before buying it, so it is important to take the best and most representative photographs you can.

Can you share any advice for other crafters who are looking to take excellent product photographs at home or on a budget?

Natural light. I love the look of natural light, particularly on a clean background. Make sure the background is not too busy and that the focal point of your photograph is the product and not a prop. Also don't be afraid to really get into your product photography physically. Try lying down or get at eye level for some photos, or even try getting above your product on a stepstool to get a bird's-eye view of it. You might be surprised by the results you get.

What do you know now that would have made photographing your toys and dealing with digital images easier for you in the beginning?

I wish I had read my camera's manual a bit earlier. I think it would have saved much frustration and time if I had invested an hour or two upfront getting acquainted with my camera.

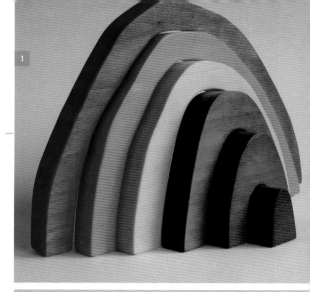

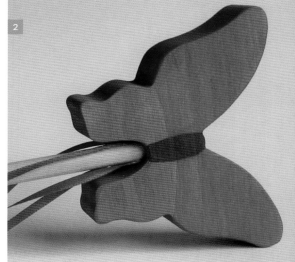

Shop name
Imagination Kids

Website
www.imaginationkidstoys.com

Make and model of camera
Canon PowerShot SD780 IS

Most used camera settings
1/60 sec, f/3.8, ISO 400, 5.9mm

Most used camera/lighting accessories
None

Favorite time of day to shoot
Mid-afternoon

Favorite location
Somewhere with indirect/diffused natural light

What has been the best photography-related lesson or tip you have received?
Take more photos than you think you need from as many different angles as possible when doing a product shoot. You will never wish you had taken fewer photos, but if you skimp on the shots, there is a good chance you will wish you had just taken a few more.

[1] Rainbow Stacker Toy
Canon PowerShot SD780 IS
1/30 sec, f/3.8, ISO 400, 5.9mm

[2] Red and Pink Butterfly Wand
Canon PowerShot SD780 IS
1/60 sec, f/3.8, ISO 400, 5.9mm

All products manufactured and photographed by *Erin Freuchtel-Dearing*

Planning & Setting Up

There are so many reasons why customers should buy your beautifully crafted ceramics over the mass-produced pieces they find at the mall. If your photographs show your workmanship and the distinctive details of your product, using soft lighting and sharp detail shots, they'll be selling like hotcakes.

Suggested camera modes:

→ Macro
→ Nighttime with the flash turned off if you're working with candlelight
→ Portrait
→ Aperture priority
→ Manual

Helpful equipment:

→ Seamless white background or light tent
→ Tripod
→ Reflector
→ Manufacturing tools and materials

[1] Small Porcelain Tea Light Holders with Hearts
Nikon D3
1/160 sec, f/2.8, ISO 1250, 50mm
Wendy Jung

[2] Hand-thrown Light Pendants
Nikon D3
1/160 sec, f/2.8, ISO 1250, 50mm
Lisa Warninger

[3] Planter Trio
Canon EOS 5D
1/60 sec, f/4, ISO 400, 47mm
Becky McNeel

ARTIFICIAL LIGHTING OPTION: CANDLES

Candles immediately relax a scene. They are cheap, easy to find, and create a soft and sensual mood. They are ideal for use in the products where they will eventually belong, such as ceramic candleholders/covers and lamps. They are also perfect for deliberately low-lit scenes to bring a sense of warmth and coziness. Select a time of day when the sun has set but it is not yet too dark. Keep the flash turned off and use a tripod for stability. "Expose the scene" (get your settings right) before you light the candles. The tripod will allow you to use a lower shutter setting and this will help to allow in more light. Remember from exposure and histograms on pages 20 and 21 that a purposely low-lit scene will be weighted to the left of the histogram, so if it looks a little too dark, that is okay. A suitable white balance for candlelight is around 2000K, which is similar to sunrise and sunset, if your camera has a preset for either of those. Otherwise, try auto white balance (learn more on page 22). Light your candles and reshoot.

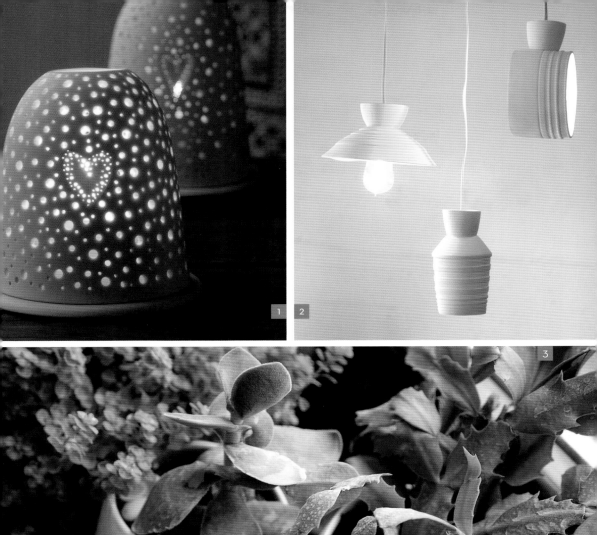

1 | 2

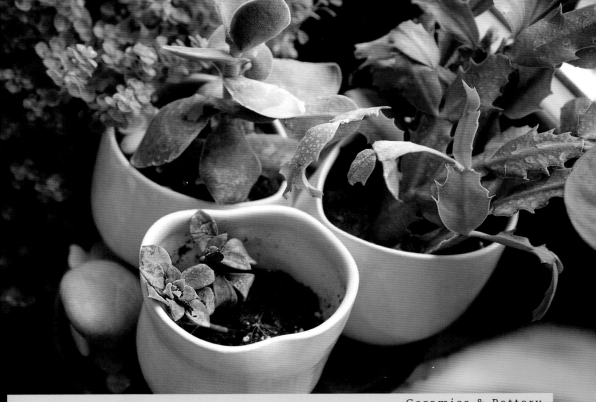

3

Ceramics & Pottery

Composition

BACKGROUNDS

Neutral

Even if your products are transparent, subtly colored, white or black, they still speak to the customer about their texture, shape, and features, both inside and out, so a neutral background will allow them to do so without distraction.

Color

Use a large aperture setting so that the background is blurred and, therefore, not too distracting.

In situ

You're dedicated to making beautiful products for use in the home and garden, and styling them in that way is very motivating to customers, giving them ideas for where to put your product and what to do with it.

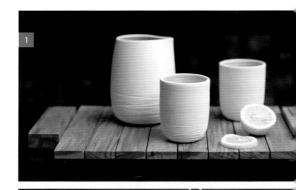

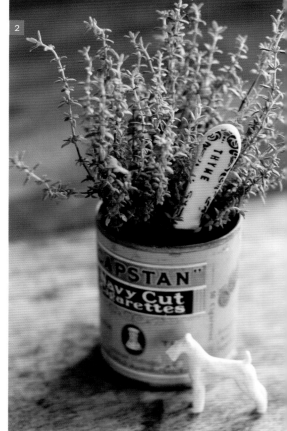

[1] **Scribble Pitcher and Tumblers**
Nikon D3
1/800 sec, f/2.5, ISO 400, 50mm
Lisa Warninger

[2] **Thyme Garden Label**
Canon EOS Digital Rebel XSi
1/125 sec, f/2.8, ISO 80, 50mm
Alarna Zinn

FRAMING & VIEWPOINT

You are familiar with your product from top to bottom, but your customer is not. Shoot your product from all angles to display the most interesting features.

Position your product in the middle of the frame, but allow slightly more room at the top. This will make the product seem like it is right in front of your customer and not hovering above or below. Staggering a selection of your products in one frame can look very artistic and interesting.

Take one of your photographs and count how many elements you can see. Count every feature of your product—color, texture, shine, pattern, etc.—and your setting—wall, floor, skirting board, shadow, window, etc. There is no set number for the right or wrong amount of elements, and many will be subtle, but it will give you an idea of just how much there is for your customer to look at.

PROPS, SCALE & STYLING

Capitalize on your extensive product range by using more of your own products as props. Showing more than one of a product is a delight to your customers' senses: if they like your product, they'll love seeing ten of them.

If your product is meant to have something in it, e.g., a vase, adding one or two simple flowers can be effective, but only if your setting is simple. Every color, texture, shape, and shadow in your photograph is a new element. To draw in your customers and keep them browsing your product range, you must keep it simple.

Arrange for a friend or local photographer to take photographs of you in action. The process of bringing your products to life might be unexciting to you, but to a customer it is wonderful. This shows your customers that they are investing in, not only a handmade product, but also your creativity, time, and small business as a whole. Don't be shy!

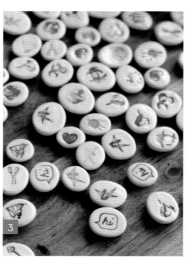

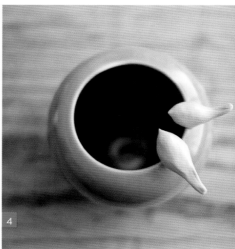

[3] Ceramic Magnets
Canon EOS Digital Rebel XSi
1/125 sec, f/2.8, ISO 80, 50mm
Alarna Zinn

[4] Lovebirdies Vase
Nikon D300
1/125 sec, f/1.4, ISO 250, 30mm
Christine Tenenholtz

Common Problems & FAQs

Q. How do I show the delicate nature of my ceramics/pottery?
Conveying delicacy is all about soft light. Backlighting (page 12) is a very popular technique when it comes to product photography, as the gradual tapering off of the background creates a dreamy look. If you're shooting outside to maximize light and space, you may have to add in a diffuser to soften the shadows (see page 137) and use a high shutter speed. Read through the technique described for showing detail and texture of fashion and fabrics on page 73 and take a similar approach. High-contrast white or black is not delicate and will fight with your product for attention. A soft, white background is ideal to show delicacy.

Q. I bought a DSLR to take better photographs, but I'm still quite scared of the manual mode on my camera and unsure where to start with it.
An understanding of how a camera turns light into a photograph will help—read back through light, aperture, shutter, and exposure (pages 10–21). Relax (you won't hurt the camera and it won't hurt you), turn your camera to manual mode and try a random combination of settings, e.g., 1/100 sec, f/5.6, and ISO 100. Halfway press the shutter button, look for the exposure meter and, depending on the reading (it will either be underexposed, overexposed, or ideal), adjust the settings to allow in more or less light. If the camera tells you that those settings are overexposing the image, you can increase the shutter speed, and/or decrease the aperture and/or ISO. If you want to keep the shutter fast to avoid camera shake, adjust the aperture and/or ISO. If you want to keep a large depth-of-field to show as much of your product as possible, adjust the shutter and/or ISO. Give it a try, as the manual setting allows you full control over light into your camera and will help to create a photograph that reflects more accurately what you can see with your eyes.

Q. I'm not sure whether to show my bowls full of food or empty. Which approach is best?
There is no right or wrong answer to this question, as it is quite subjective. Many stylists keep products looking new and unused in photographs, and others include things like food in a bowl as a prop to inspire and show scale. Certain objects look great when photographed, such as fruit and vegetables, but there are also some that don't look so great. Less is definitely more, so if you're unsure, leave the bowl empty.

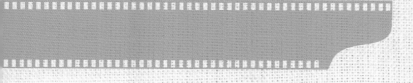

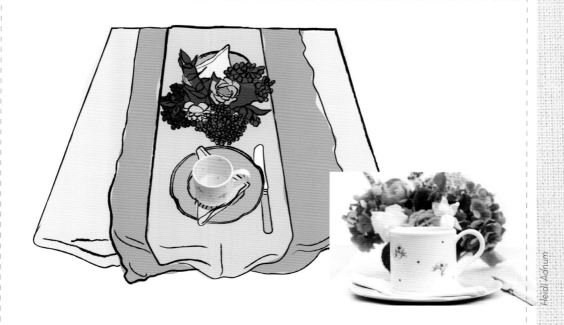

Heidi Adnum

Q. How can I style a photograph like the professionals?
You don't have to rent a fancy studio or hire a stylist to produce beautiful photographs. Use a sturdy table and, depending on the finish of your table and the look you desire, cover with fabric or card stock. Layering different colors and/or textures can look very luxurious. Position your camera close to your product to fill as much of the frame as you can with it. Showing a hint of your thoughtful styling and props, such as only half of a vase of flowers or the handle of a knife is enough to get the message across while still keeping the styling and props in the back seat. Don't obscure too much of your product with your props and styling. After all, you want the workmanship to be clearly visible. Stabilizing your camera using a tripod (see page 64) makes styling a little easier, as, once you've found the right angle, you can leave your camera where it is and move your props around, taking sample shots after each change to see the effects and decide on your favorite look. If you're having trouble deciding which props to use and how, exactly, to style your product, remember to keep it simple. Start with a table and then add in things one at a time.

Practitioner Spotlight
Clair Catillaz

How do you take photographs that show off your ceramics so beautifully?
It's a continuous learning process. Since I sell my work on www.Etsy.com, I can easily see what people respond to. Sometimes it seems that the photograph is even more important than the item itself! It's important to not only show off the object for sale, but also convey a sense of the overall brand.

Has your photographic process changed the way you make your ceramics?
Not really, but it definitely helps to have some beautiful new photos to keep me inspired. It's amazing how a professional-looking photograph can make me feel more like a professional artist.

How do you show accurate color, along with detail and texture in your photographs?
Color can be tricky, especially due to the variation in computer monitors. I adjust my white balance when shooting, and I'll tweak colors in post-production, as needed.

What has been your biggest photographic challenge?
Setting up shots in a way that involves a minimal amount of editing. I'd rather take more photos than push pixels around. Also, the issue of reflection is a big one. There's nothing worse than seeing your own face in the side of a teapot.

Was there a point when product photography got easier for you? If so, when and why?
Finding a good spot to shoot in! I use a table and a wall with natural, non-direct light. Also, disciplining myself to use a tripod for every shoot. Sounds basic, but I used to skip this all the time and then wonder why my photos looked bad.

What are common mistakes people make when it comes to photographing ceramics and pottery?
Making things look too gallery-like. My work belongs in the kitchen, or on the dining-room table, so my photos need a warm and inviting feel.

Can you share any advice on taking excellent product photographs at home or on a budget?
All you really need is a tripod, a roll of butcher paper, a camera that has some manual function, and a little bit of patience. Styling is important, but keep it simple. If you have a good product and good light, you can take a beautiful photograph.

What do you know now that would have made photographing your ceramics and dealing with digital images easier for you in the beginning?
How to use Adobe Photoshop! I'm still no expert, but learning the basics made everything easier.

What has been the best photography-related lesson or tip you have received?
Spend time at the start to set up a shoot. Compose shots to avoid cropping later. Cover that scratch in the table. If the light is wrong, wait until tomorrow.

Shop name
CLAM LAB

Website
www.clamlab.com

Make and model of camera
Canon EOS Digital Rebel XSi

Most used camera settings
Manual

Most used camera/lighting accessories
Tripod

Favorite time of day to shoot
Any time with good daylight, so shooting hours can be shorter in the winter. I find it's easiest to use only natural, indirect/diffused light, especially since my glazes are reflective

Favorite location
In my kitchen or bedroom, depending on where the light looks best on that particular day

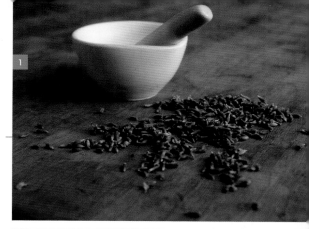

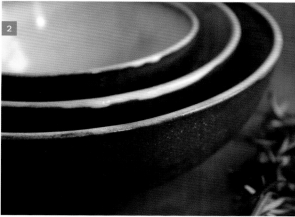

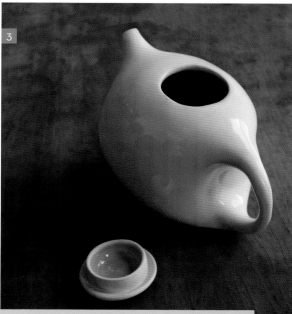

[1] Mini Mortar and Pestle Set
Canon EOS Digital Rebel XSi
1/20 sec, f/5.6, ISO 400, 29mm

[2] Chocolate Nesting Bowl Set
Canon EOS Digital Rebel XSi
1/15 sec, f/5.6, ISO 400, 55mm

[3] Creamy Teapot
Canon EOS Digital Rebel XSi
1/20 sec, f/5.6, ISO 400, 20mm

All products manufactured and photographed by *Clair Catillaz*

Ceramics & Pottery

Planning & Setting Up

As well as showing customers the style, detail, and features of your artwork, take the opportunity to show them how beautiful your creations will look in their home. Inspire them with subtle suggestions for how to use and enjoy your artwork.

Suggested camera modes:
→ Landscape
→ Portrait
→ Macro
→ Program with low ISO
→ Aperture priority
→ Shutter priority
→ Manual

Helpful equipment:
→ Tripod
→ Reflector
→ Flash diffuser
→ Seamless white background/light tent

ARTIFICIAL LIGHTING OPTION: LARGE WORK LIGHTS

If your artwork is large or you simply cannot gather enough light for your photography, take a trip to your local hardware or electrical store. They should sell portable work lights and/or floodlights, which are usually powered by simply connecting their cord to an electrical main's socket. They are available with daylight/white bulbs, and some have replaceable bulbs, so you can replace the yellow-halogen bulbs that may come as standard. Some even come with a mount/tripod-like device, too. Investing in two of these lights could give you the flexibility of lighting from both sides and/or to create a rim light (see page 12 for more information). Diffuse the light by angling them toward a white wall or up to a white ceiling; this way the light will bounce on and off the wall/ceiling and onto your product. You can also shine them through white fabric hung in front of the light, or perhaps over a towel rack, for more diffusion. Be aware that these lights can get hot, so hanging the fabric directly over them can be a fire hazard.

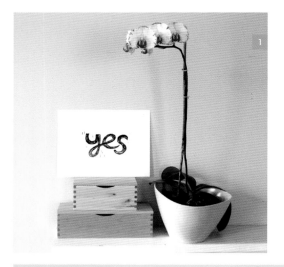

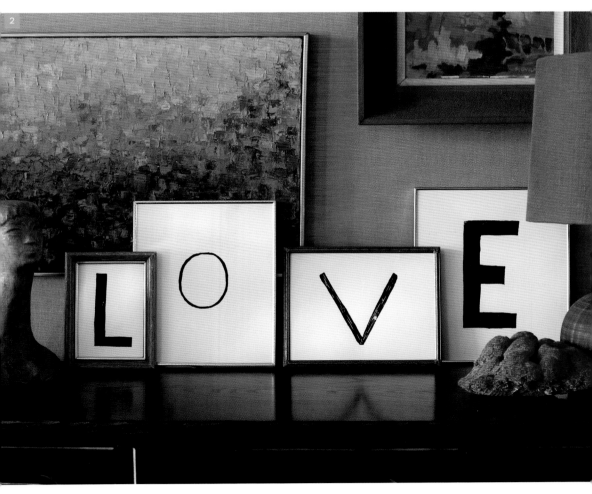

[1] Yes
Canon EOS Digital Rebel XT
1/80 sec, f/5.6, ISO 400, 18mm
Stacey Bradley

[2] Love
Canon EOS 5D
1/15 sec, f/4.5, ISO 500, 50mm
Gayle Brooker

Composition

BACKGROUNDS
Neutral
If you want your customers to focus on the art and art alone, choose a neutral background, such as a white or light-gray wall.

Color
The general rule is to select one background color and stick with it. However, if your artwork is very similar in design and, for example, only the pattern changes, you could afford a couple of different colored backgrounds in your range. Be sure to select colors in the same shade/tone that complement your work, and, if it doesn't look right, go back to one color or neutral.

In situ
Position your art around the home, or create a homey scene within your studio, to get your customers thinking about how to achieve something similar.

FRAMING & VIEWPOINT
Positioning your artwork off-center may sound like something that would cause an imbalance within your photograph, but it can have the opposite effect. This is true for many in situ scenes, where parts of other objects are shown; for example, the visible top of a side table centered in the frame with a lamp placed on its left makes the top-right of the photograph a perfect place to position your artwork.

Show a portion of your scene, such as the corner of the frame containing your print—it's a combination of showing detail and texture, and a fun little tease!

PROPS, SCALE & STYLING
Your art is making its own statement and you should keep it that way with minimal or subtle props. Bring your scene to life with one or two homely touches and a pop of color. A lifestyle scene with everyday props is also an effective way to show scale.

Try layering a few pieces of your art, if it is flat, such as photographs or prints. This helps to fill the frame and suggests ways to display and combine your work.

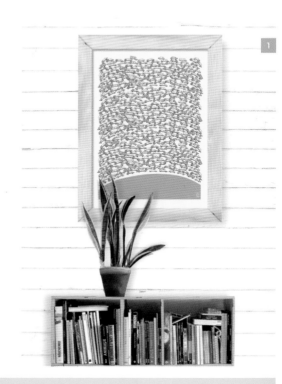

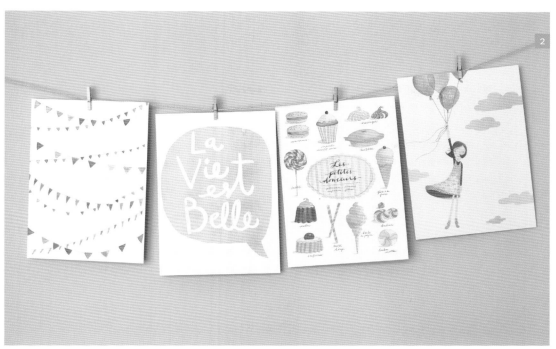

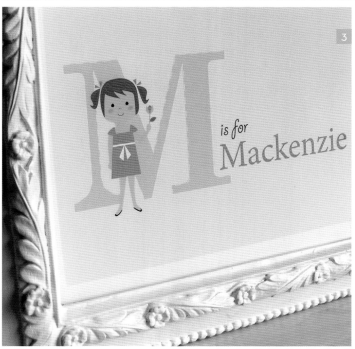

[1] Traffic Jam Print
Canon PowerShot SX110 IS
1/125 sec, f/2.8, ISO 400, 78mm
Judy Kaufmann

[2] "La vie est belle" Set
Nikon D90
1/125 sec, f/5.6, ISO 360, 38mm
Eve Legris

[3] Olliegraphic Name Print
Minolta DiMAGE Z1
1/100 sec, f/4.5, ISO 50, 9.7mm
Meg Bartholomy

Common Problems & FAQs

Q. I'm bored of photographing my prints alone in a frame on the wall. What else can I try?
You can try asking someone to hold the print in his or her hands. Remember to position your model in front of a neutral or complementary background and shoot from straight on. Focus in on the artwork and not the model.

An approach sometimes overlooked in photography of art, prints especially, is getting up close. This shows texture, color and, to your customer, is like being able to stand right in front of your product. When we get up-close and personal with a piece of art, there's a load of information present that's a real treat for the eyes.

Think also about your inspiration for the artwork. If you can include some of this in the scene, it reveals to your customers more about your creative process, and they are bound to find this interesting and inspiring.

Q. There's a big, gray shadow under my product and it looks awful in the photograph. Help!
Shadows are normal, but dark, harsh shadows are distracting. They are the result of a hard light, so, a light source that seems small from the point of view of your product. Get rid of harsh shadows by diffusing the light and turning hard light into soft light. Your photography will improve by leaps and bounds when you start to read the shadows.

Q. How do I avoid reflection in the glass in front of my artwork?
Reflection is a normal feature of photographs and makes objects look real by adding dimension. Most of the time, reflection isn't something you should worry about removing or avoiding. There are times, however, when it isn't helpful and is distracting, such as the glare or reflection from the glass in eyeglasses or in front of framed artwork. Reflection occurs when a light source bounces onto a reflective surface, such as glass, and then into the lens. The best way to avoid reflection on artwork behind glass is to simply remove the glass. If that isn't possible, then:
→ position the object at an angle to the light source so that the reflective surface is no longer reflecting light directly into the lens;
→ light the artwork from the side; and/or
→ move your camera to another angle, one that isn't picking up the reflection, and, for framed artwork, usually slightly underneath or to one side works just fine.

Q. I can't remove the glass, move the print, or change the direction of the light/product. What else can I do to avoid reflection?

If you have tried avoiding reflection in glass using the techniques we've just talked about but you'd prefer to shoot straight on to your product, what you need to do is use what is often called a "gobo." Gobos are things that "go between" the object and the item being reflected, such as the light or the photographer. A non-reflective gobo, such as a sheet of black card, can be held up somewhere between you and the artwork to minimize reflection. You may have to move the gobo around until you can no longer see a reflection when looking through the camera. You may also have to use more than one gobo.

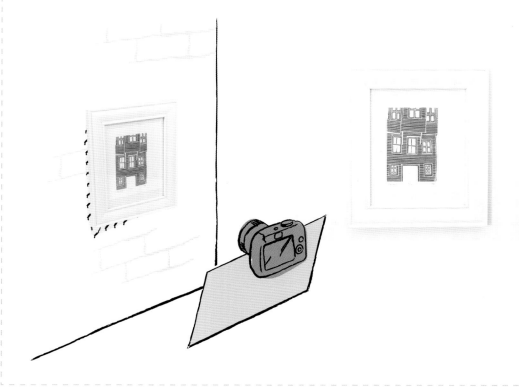

Heidi Adnum

Practitioner Spotlight
Stacey Bradley

How do you take photographs that show off your art so beautifully?
I like to put my work in a clean, modern environment, as I think it works best, and I take a lot of photos at a lot of angles!

How do you show accurate color, along with detail and texture, in your photographs?
I take close-up shots using as much natural light as possible.

What has been your biggest photographic challenge?
Learning how to edit the images.

Can you tell us if there was a point when product photography got easier for you?
Once I had a professional photographer friend give me some simple tips and take some photographs for me. Afterward, I had learned a lot and felt so much more confident. There are so many tutorials out there. Study them—it makes a big difference!

What do you think are common mistakes people make when it comes to photographing art?
Not placing the product in a lifestyle environment. This doesn't show the product as it could (or would) be used.

Can you share any advice for other crafters who are looking to take excellent product photographs at home or on a budget?
Play around with the camera and setup as much as possible, until you feel you've got the best possible photograph with the equipment available.

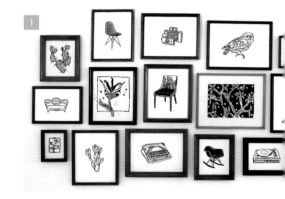

[1] Linoleum Block Prints
Canon EOS 5D
1/6 sec, f/8, ISO 400, 42mm
Gayle Brooker

What do you know now that would have made photographing your art and dealing with digital images easier for you in the beginning?
Editing. Even the slightest tweak can brighten or sharpen an image.

What has been the best photography-related lesson or tip you have received?
Not photographing my framed work with the glass in it! And learning about white balance has been invaluable.

Shop name
Perla Anne

Website
www.perlaanne.etsy.com

Make and model of camera
Canon EOS Digital Rebel XT

Most used camera settings
Automatic

Most used camera/lighting accessories
None

Favorite time of day to shoot
Morning to midday

Favorite location
Home, studio, or friends with an interesting home environment

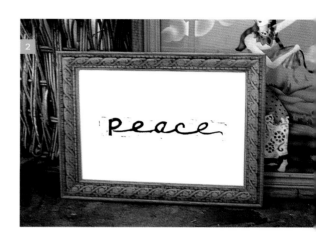

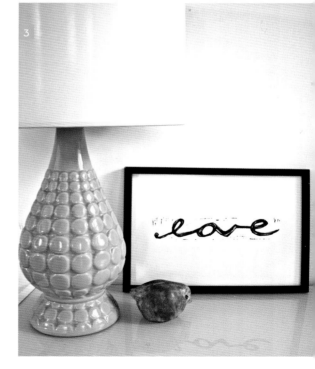

[2] Peace
Canon EOS Digital Rebel XT
1/30 sec, f/3.5, ISO 400, 18mm
Stacey Bradley

[3] Love
Canon EOS Digital Rebel XT
1/40 sec, f/4, ISO 400, 18mm
Stacey Bradley

Planning & Setting Up

Not only do your customers want to buy your product for its functionality, they may want it for its beauty and coffee-table appeal. This opens wide your options with photography, as long as you keep your product as the clear and obvious focus of the photograph.

Suggested camera modes:
→ Portrait
→ Macro
→ Aperture priority
→ Manual

Helpful equipment:
→ Tripod
→ Reflector
→ Colored background

Remember that soft, natural lighting needs to be your first choice. Try everything you can to maximize and enlarge a small, hard light source. If all else fails, you can achieve good lighting by using artificial lights, many of which can be found around the home.

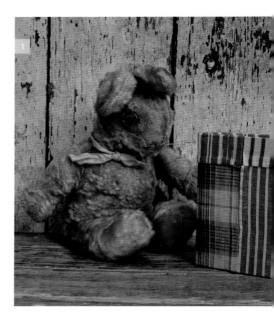

ARTIFICIAL LIGHTING OPTION: HOUSEHOLD LAMPS

Lighting with household lamps is very straightforward, as long as you don't combine them with other artificial light sources, and you do set the white balance to lamp, tungsten, or auto, their color can sometimes warm up a scene. Modern, energy-saving bulbs are usually more white or daylight-balanced than the older tungsten bulbs, so check the pack for confirmation. Lampshades act as built-in diffusers, so if you've already got a white lampshade, you've already got a useful diffuser. Position the lamp out-of-frame by placing it to the side of your product.

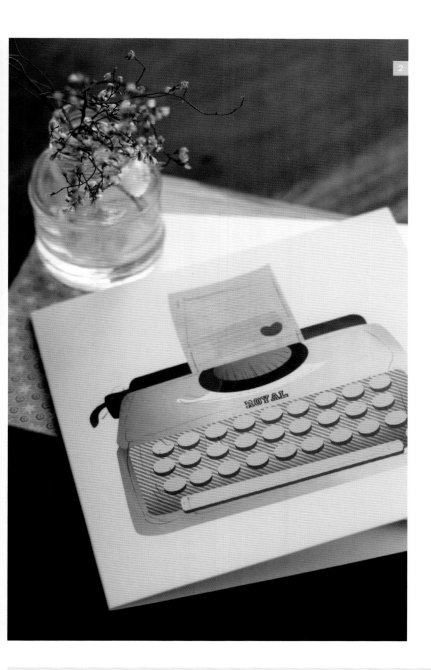

[1] Travel Journal
Nikon D70
1/80 sec, f5.6,
ISO 200, 28mm
Peg and Awl

**[2] With Love
Greetings Card**
Canon EOS Digital
Rebel XSi
1/125 sec, f/4,
ISO 80, 50mm
Alarna Zinn

Composition

BACKGROUNDS
Neutral
Books, magazines, and stationery products are similar to art in that they have a lot going on. They're telling their own story through pattern, color, text, texture, and shape. So, keeping the background neutral will help to let them take center stage. A light tent is ideal (page 54).

Color
If your product range has a color theme, then a colored background could really set off your product (see page 45).

Textured
Aged wood makes a glorious contrast to neat and tidy books/magazines/stationery. Fabric also offers an interesting, subtle contrast.

Consider using your own product as a textured background, too. It acts as a neutral background in a way, as the matching colors, shapes, and textures don't distract the eye. Choose between blurring the background versus keeping the background in sharp focus (page 16). Blurring the background keeps the overall look of the photograph quite soft and gentle, with the focus on the product at the front of the frame. Keeping all products in clear focus can look bold and impressive. There's no right or wrong way, it just depends on what look you prefer.

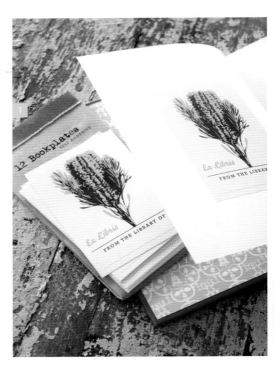

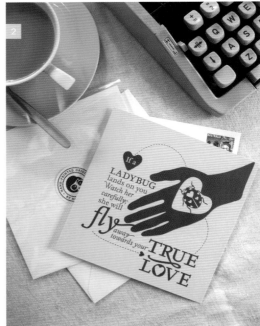

[1] Nora Whynot Banksia Bookplates
Canon EOS
Digital Rebel XSi
0.4 sec, f/9,
ISO 200, 50mm
Nora Whynot

[2] Nora Whynot Old Wives' Tale True Love Card
Canon EOS
Digital Rebel XSi
1/60 sec, f/6.3,
ISO 400, 50mm
Nora Whynot

[3] Baker's Twine Sample Pack
Canon PowerShot
SD1000
1/100 sec, f/2.8,
ISO 400, 5.8mm
Kristy Risser

[4] Nora Whynot Perpetual Calendar
Canon EOS
Digital Rebel XSi
1/80 sec, f/5.6,
ISO 100, 50mm
Nora Whynot

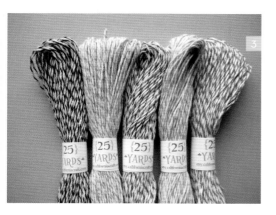

FRAMING & VIEWPOINT

Centering your product in the middle of the frame works nicely for books, magazines, and stationery. It boldly presents them to your customer.

Deliberately cropping out a portion of your product (e.g., showing two-thirds of your product peeking up from the bottom of the frame) can be fun and powerful.

To show someone reading your book or magazine, shoot from above and over his or her shoulder.

PROPS, SCALE & STYLING

Showing your product in action, such as tape on a box, is practical and also shows scale, pattern, and usability. Look around outside for objects that could become backgrounds, such as chairs, tables, wood stumps, and pieces of garden equipment, especially if your product can be used outside the home, like a calendar.

Objects that also tie in with your genre and that can convey scale are pencils, string, and envelopes. Create a scene that your customers would love to come home to. Fresh flowers are a nice touch.

Common Problems & FAQs

Q. I struggle to make my books/magazines/stationery look interesting in photographs. They are thin and flat, and I don't know how to style them. What can I do?

The best way to make products seem bigger and make more of an impact is to photograph them from slightly below eye-level or straight on. Do this by standing up your book/magazine/stationery (if it won't stand up on its own, sit something heavy, such as a mug, out of shot and behind it) and positioning your camera at the same level as your product. You can also lay your product down flat and photograph it from above to get a similar effect. Grouping your products together will also make them look more interesting. You can add interest by creating a beautiful scene that your customers would want to replicate in their home.

Q. The clear plastic packaging I use for my books/magazines/stationery causes glare/reflection in the photograph. Is there any way to avoid this?

The best way to avoid reflection is to remove the plastic covering. If you can't do this, or need one photograph to show your product in its packaging, you have three options:

→ Position your product so that it is not directly facing the light.
   You can light your product from the side or from behind.
→ Photograph from an angle where the reflection is not visible
   (e.g., from the side or from slightly underneath).
→ Place a gobo between your product and the reflection.
   (Read up on avoiding reflection/glare and making a gobo on page 121.)

Q. I use a travel tripod to shoot but it's always falling over. Is there anything I can do to fix it?

Around the house or at the studio you can weigh down the tripod with a heavy object, such as a bag of rice. Outside, or on location, multitask and weigh down the tripod with a bag containing drinks and/or snacks. Larger, more expensive and professional tripods are heavier and, therefore, less prone to falling over, so keep that in mind for when you are next upgrading equipment. No matter what size or cost your tripod, however, if what you are putting on it is too heavy, or if the legs are imbalanced, it will be bound to fall.

Q. I'm using window light but it's still quite harsh, causing dark shadows. What can I do?

You can tape a sheet of white paper to the window, or draw across a white, sheer curtain. If possible, wait a while until the sun is lower, or at a different position in the sky, when it is more likely to be reflected light and not direct light. Window light doesn't have to be bright and strong to create a beautiful photograph.

Q. I notice colored backgrounds are used a lot in editorial shoots and would love to achieve the same effect. How is it done?

Creating your own colored background couldn't be easier: Choose a piece of nonshine card in a complementary color and tape it to the wall. Place your product on a neutral or complementary-colored base in front of the card and shoot. Be sure that you frame or crop out any space where the background drops off, for example, at the sides of the card or the edge of your chair or table.

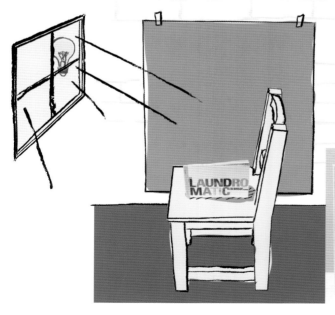

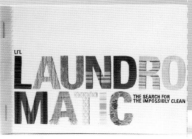

Practitioner Spotlight
Anna Bond

How do you take photographs that show off your paper goods and designs so beautifully?

I really love clean, simple photographs, especially since our products are bright and colorful. I don't want my environment to compete with them, so I photograph on a white piece of paper and edit the shots in Adobe Photoshop to give them a crisp, bright look.

How do you show accurate color, along with detail and texture, in your photographs?

Sometimes it's tough to get the color just right with the camera, so I almost always tweak my photos in post-production to be sure the true colors are coming through. It's important that the online customer is getting an accurate depiction of the quality of our goods. To ensure the best detail, I use a tripod to be sure the shots are in focus and not blurry.

What has been your biggest photographic challenge?

My biggest challenge can be editing the photos so that the true colors come through and all the photos look consistent, even if they've been taken at different times. I've learned how to use Adobe Photoshop to bring my photos to life.

Can you tell us if there was a point when product photography got easier for you?

I think I'm used to it more now, so in that sense it's easier. I know what to expect and what the process will be like. I feel like over time I've found a bit of a rhythm to it.

What do you think are common mistakes when it comes to photographing paper goods?

I don't think some people realize the importance of great photos. To me, they can make or break sales, and affect whether or not you come across as professional. Even if you don't have a great camera, you can work with what you have. When in doubt, just go simple with a white background and take the photos outside in the sun, if you don't have good enough lights to use indoors.

Can you share any advice for other crafters/ bloggers who are looking to take excellent product photographs at home or on a budget?

Invest in the best camera you can (or borrow or rent one) and photograph against a simple, light-colored background. Use photo-editing software to make sure the photos are consistent and your colors look great. If you still don't feel comfortable, I recommend taking a local photography class.

What do you know now that would have made photographing your product and dealing with digital images easier for you in the beginning?

Learning about your camera and editing software is one of the biggest steps. If you know how to use your tools, it will make your life much easier. I took photography in high school and used vintage manual cameras for years, and I feel that helped me to understand how to take better photos.

What has been the best photography-related lesson or tip you have received?

Ask for help if you need it! Take a class, shadow a photographer, read up on tips, and practice. Often the best way to learn is by practicing, so experiment until you're happy with the results.

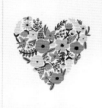
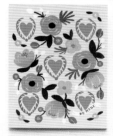

Shop name
Rifle Paper Co.

Website
www.riflepaperco.com

Make and model of camera
Nikon D80

Most used camera settings
Manual settings with lowest possible ISO (to reduce noise/grain)

Most used camera/lighting accessories
Sunlight, tripod

Favorite time of day to shoot
Early afternoon

Favorite location
The front of our studio space where the light is best

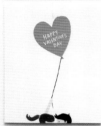
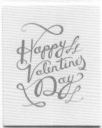

[1] Assorted Valentine's Day Set
Nikon D80
1/25 sec, f/4.2, ISO 200, 32mm

[2] Assorted Holiday Gift Tags
Nikon D80
1/30 sec, f/4.5, ISO 200, 38mm

[3] Scottie Card
Nikon D80
1/50 sec, f/5, ISO 400, 32mm

All products manufactured and photographed by *Rifle Paper Co.*

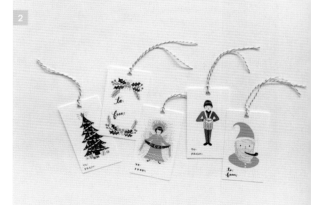
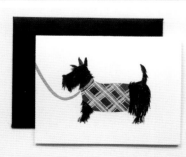

Planning & Setting Up

You know that your product would look great in your customers' homes; you just have to show them! Keep things simple and clean, and let your product do all the talking.

Suggested camera modes:
→ Landscape
→ Program with low ISO
→ Shutter priority
→ Manual

Helpful equipment:
→ Tripod
→ Flash diffuser
→ Off-camera daylight-balanced lighting

ARTIFICIAL LIGHTING OPTION: CAR HEADLIGHTS

Large home accessories, such as furniture, can be lit with car headlights. Yes, you read that correctly, car headlights. The best way to use car headlights as a light source is as fill light (see more on page 15). Naturally, this is going to work in outdoor settings or in the garage. Once you've set up your scene, move your car toward or away from your product. The further away it is, the less powerful the light will become.

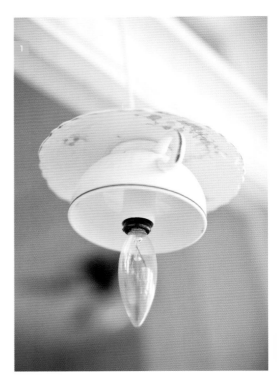

[1] Teacup Light
Canon EOS 5D MkII
1/80 sec, f/2.8, ISO 500, 50mm
Tytie

[2] Mountains Tea Towels
Canon EOS 5D
1/30 sec, f/5, ISO 400, 32mm
Fine Little Day

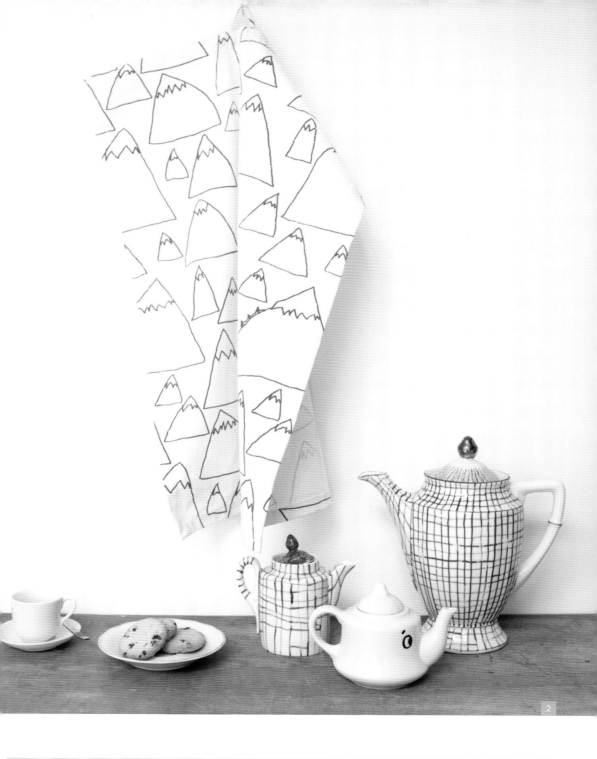

Composition

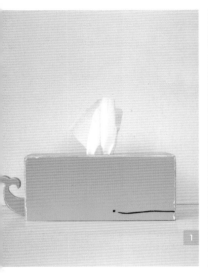

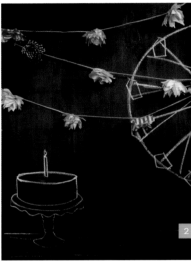

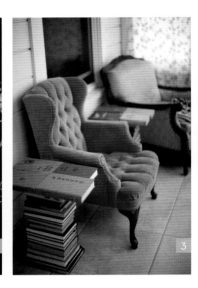

BACKGROUNDS
Neutral
Seamless white backgrounds are the ultimate in simple, clean, and neutral backgrounds (page 62) and they can be perfect to display home accessories. If your home accessory products are on the smaller side, use a light tent (page 54) for the same effect.

[1] Whale Tissue Holder
Canon PowerShot A540
1/160 sec, f/4.5, ISO 200, 15mm
A Sparkly Pony

[2] Flower Garland
Canon PowerShot G10
1/8 sec, f/2.8, ISO 400, 6.7mm
Pretty Swell

[3] Book End Tables
Canon EOS 5D MkII
1/400 sec, f/2.8, ISO 500, 50mm
Tytie

For a dark, neutral background, use a blackboard, as they are a flattering almost-black color. They don't have to be brand-new or unused.

In situ
Look for locations around your home and garden, especially in less obvious places, such as the kitchen or bathroom, windowsills, and garden sheds.

If you're stuck for inspiration, visit your local thrift store where you may find some props, such as vintage chairs and tables.

An in situ background is a superb choice for products that have been re-purposed. It shows customers exactly how to use a familiar product in an unfamiliar way.

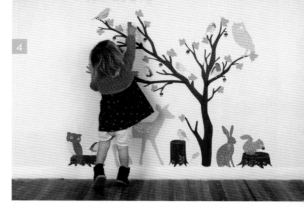

[4] Reusable Fabric Wall Decals
Canon EOS 30D
1/125 sec, f/5.6, ISO 100, 50mm
Mae

[5] Kitchen Conversions Tea Towels
Canon EOS Digital Rebel T1i
1/64 sec, f/5, ISO 100, 50mm
Sweet Fine Day

[6] Ohoy Wallpaper
Canon EOS 5D
1/60 sec, f/4, ISO 320, 38mm
Fine Little Day

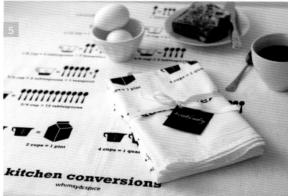

FRAMING & VIEWPOINT

Turn your product to one side, if you would like to show more detail, and shoot from various angles to gain different perspectives.

If you are shooting large objects that are particularly difficult to fit within the camera frame, such as furniture and toys, try shooting from above. This will make the object look smaller and will show more of its features and the scene as a whole. Use a stepladder if necessary.

PROPS, SCALE & STYLING

Models make great props for home accessories; it's very easy to shoot them using your product and looking comfortable, as they have something to focus on and tend to forget (maybe just a little) that they are being photographed. They also show scale and ways to use the product.

Fresh fruit, vegetables, and other food, crockery, and furniture are just a few of the many suitable props to show scale and style for home accessories. Artwork is also a great choice for a prop.

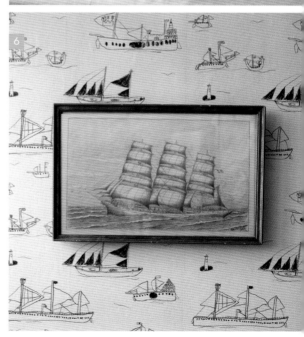

Common Problems & FAQs

Q. My home accessories would look great photographed in a beautiful home. Problem is, though, I live in a tiny, less-than-photogenic apartment. Help!

Make large aperture settings your friend, as these will create a blurred background and then it isn't obvious what environment you're shooting in. Even just including the corner of a mantelpiece in a photograph can create the illusion of an opulent (or even just appropriate) setting. If all else fails, though, approach your friends; there's bound to be someone you know with a larger house, with more space and natural light. Failing that, try a local guesthouse; they may allow you time to shoot in their home and garden in return for some of your products or a credit on your website or product listing. You could do the same at a local not-for-profit heritage home or garden in return for a charitable donation.

Q. I simply don't want to shoot outside in the winter but it's dark inside. What can I do?

Go on the hunt for large windows and shoot with your product positioned near to them. You can also try some of the techniques to maximize light and the artificial lighting options mentioned in this book. Failing that, the best thing you can do is cover up, go outside, and try your best. Wintertime can be the perfect elixir for product photography because there's no blazing sunlight and the natural, neutral scenes can be very attractive.

Q. What are the best props to use?

Generally, the more simply put together your photograph is, the better it will look. Styling a photograph with a home accessory is like showing a house that is for sale; it should look and feel warm and welcoming, but not too personal. Your customers want to imagine your product in their home, not yours. Edit your scene to remove distractions and meaningless information, and add back in one or two props.

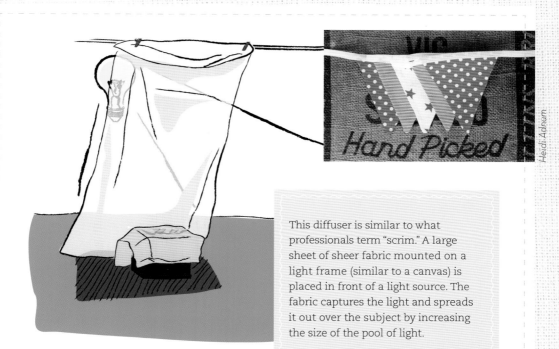

Heidi Adnam

This diffuser is similar to what professionals term "scrim." A large sheet of sheer fabric mounted on a light frame (similar to a canvas) is placed in front of a light source. The fabric captures the light and spreads it out over the subject by increasing the size of the pool of light.

Q. My products are large and it's really difficult to take nice photographs of them inside. Is there anything else I can do?

There are times when photographing objects indoors in low-light conditions is difficult. If taking them outside helps but the shadows are too harsh, position them under the clothesline (or other tall structure) and diffuse the light—it will help tremendously. Hang white fabric on the clothesline, positioning it between the sun and your setting/product. You will see that it creates a shadow on the ground. It is this shadow that you're going to shoot in. If the shadow is too small, use a larger piece of fabric. Using white fabric means that you won't cause a color-cast on your product. Creating the ideal outdoor diffuser will depend on the intensity of light. If, when you need to shoot, the sun is very strong and bright, you might need to use a thicker fabric or a few layers of fabric to increase its opacity. If the available light isn't that harsh but still causes shadows, try a white shower curtain. This technique is also very useful for photographing large size, awkwardly shaped items.

Practitioner Spotlight
William & Katie Dohman

How do you take photographs that show off your home accessories so beautifully?

Since our items are home décor pieces, we try to stage them in a way that helps customers envision what they might look like in their own home. It's less like a product shot and more like an editorial environment. We set the mood and sell for a lifestyle. When you want to see just an item or its detail, it's great to shoot on white or solid background, but it doesn't have the same wow factor for us as a magazine spread.

Has your photographic process changed the way you make your products?

Yes. We've made several pieces that look great when you move around them and in real life, but photographing them never highlighted the pieces as they are. As a result, we didn't have great success with those sales online, even though we were crazy about the design. Online you can't experience the products in three dimensions. We bear that in mind and think about what works best online versus pieces that might fare better at art shows and shops.

What has been your biggest photographic challenge?

The brick wall we use as a background, which is also our greatest strength. It highlights some pieces really well, but with certain colors the brick clashes or pulls attention away from the item. We want to be able to change that color occasionally but we can't, so we're considering creating false walls we can paint and dress up as we wish.

Can you tell us if there was a point when product photography got easier for you?

When we upgraded to a higher-level DSLR it wasn't as much of an uphill battle. It's a huge investment of time and energy, but it's worth it. Relying on photo-editing software won't always solve your technical problems but sometimes you need tools at your fingertips. Finding time to produce great photographs is a challenge.

What do you think are common mistakes when it comes to photographing home accessories?

Photographs that are poorly lit, that are out-of-focus, and/or shot from a poor vantage point.

Can you share any advice for other crafters who are looking to take excellent product photographs at home or on a budget?

If you simply want a white background, using a light tent is an inexpensive way to light your products in a consistently nice way. If you see an image you like, look at it and figure out why you like it. Your photography is your currency, and it's worth an investment in equipment, or at the very least, time and energy. We spend a lot of time styling and working with the items we shoot.

What do you know now that would have made photographing your products and dealing with digital images easier for you in the beginning?

We started making items in the summer when the light was great all the time. Then winter rolls along in Minnesota, and we have limited light and it doesn't look as warm or inviting. So, timing shoots is important, but can be difficult when you are a small shop and want to post things regularly. A little planning can go a long way.

Shop name
Oh Dier

Website
www.ohdier.com

Make and model of camera
Canon EOS 50D

Most used camera settings
Manual or aperture priority

Most used camera/lighting accessories
Tripod and lighting

Favorite time of day to shoot
Morning near large, east-facing windows

Favorite location
The brick walls of our loft, or any textured surface. We sometimes shoot outdoors at a local park or against the side of our building

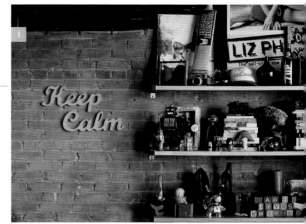

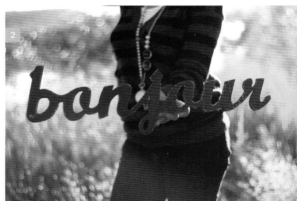

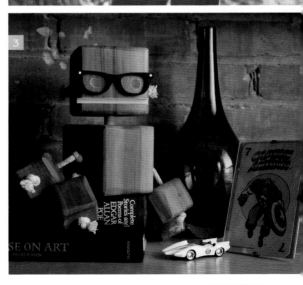

[1] Keep Calm Sign
Canon EOS 50D
1/60 sec, f/4, ISO 640, 40mm

[2] Bonjour Sign
Canon EOS 50D
1/6400 sec, f/1.8, ISO 400, 50mm

[3] William Woodsworth
Canon EOS 50D
1/30 sec, f/4.5, ISO 400, 24mm

All products manufactured and photographed by *William Dohman*

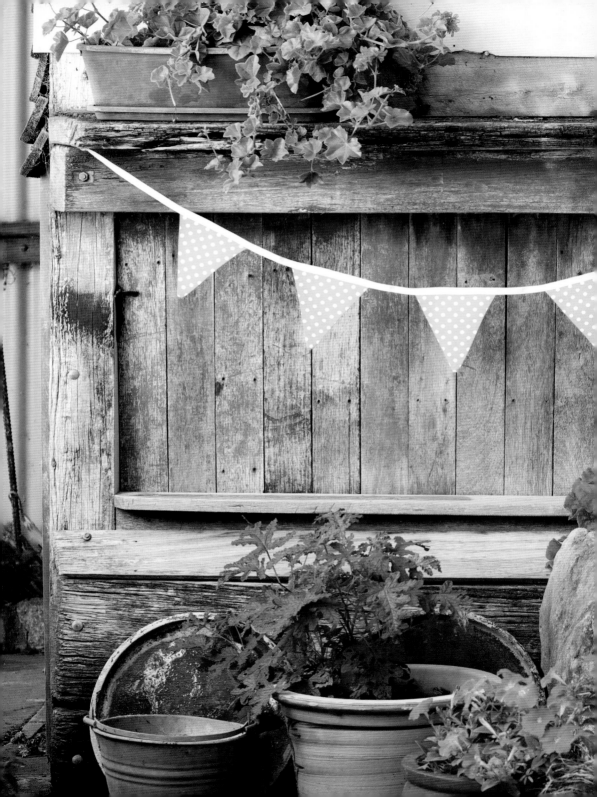

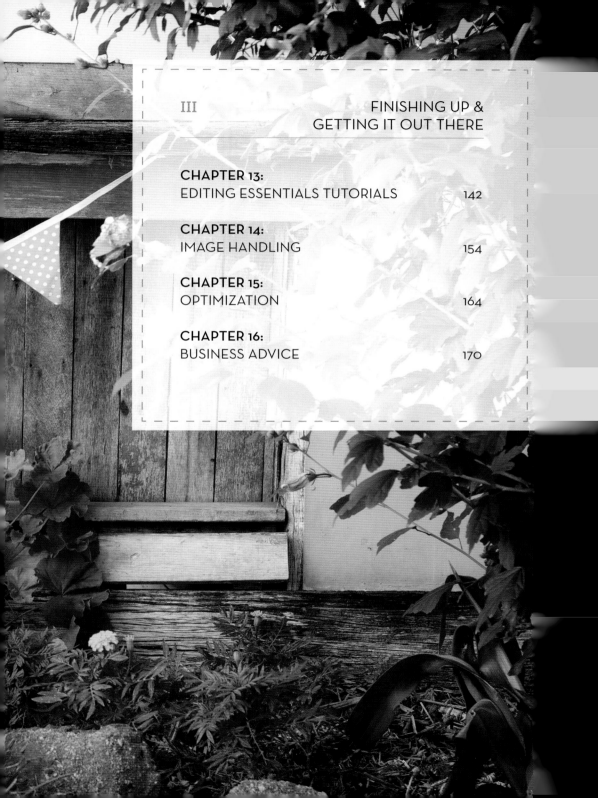

III

FINISHING UP &
GETTING IT OUT THERE

Introduction

Computer-based editing is the digital equivalent of the photographic darkroom. Also known as post-production, editing can be a highly technical and very involved process, with tons of options and effects to apply to a digital image. However, for product photography it's almost always best to keep it simple by sticking to the basics. This will help to keep your photographs looking real and will ensure you spend as little time as possible in post-production.

These tutorials have been prepared with Adobe Photoshop Elements 9, which is a less expensive, pared-back version of Adobe Photoshop. If you use different photo-editing software, don't worry: most software offers very similar (if not the same) editing tools. Refer to your software's manual and website, where you should find help to guide you through. Also try video websites such as www.youtube.com or www.vimeo.com.

You may choose to try out all of the functions in this tutorial, or simply one or two. A suggested post-production workflow is included on page 166.

Before you start editing, remember that you should always:

→ Use the camera as the primary tool to take a great photograph.
→ Create a backup of your files before editing them.
→ Spend as little time as possible in post-production, making only small changes that gently enhance the photograph and don't completely change it.

Creating a Duplicate Layer

Photoshop Elements allows you to create a copy of your image and apply any edits to that layer. This is called a duplicate layer and you can create one for every edit you apply. Doing so allows you to remove or "turn off" any edit at any stage. With all duplicate layers removed, you will see only your original, unedited image.

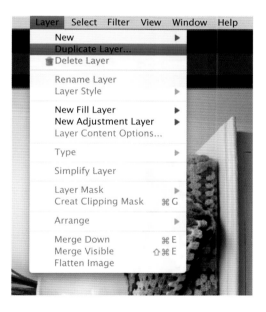

Open your image in Photoshop Elements and from the file menu click Layer > Duplicate Layer. Rename the layer and click OK.

Rotating & Cropping

This is an easy way to improve an image by removing distractions and drawing the eye to the focal point. It can also save an almost-genius image from the trash can, simply by making a slight adjustment, e.g., cropping out the problem area.

Rotating an image to be right-way-up is crucial. Product photographs that are upside-down or sideways look unprofessional. When it comes to straightening the horizontal or vertical aspect of your photograph, you can tilt the horizon slightly to make it level, or to deliberately change the angle and perspective. You can, of course, leave the horizon as it is, to convey your perspective. There's no right or wrong way, but if the contents of the photograph look lopsided or about to slide out of the frame, then straighten it up.

When you do need to crop, do it early on in the editing process: you don't want to waste time retouching only to crop out the retouched area later on. Cropping might be necessary to change the aspect ratio (the width-to-height ratio) of the image using fixed parameters. For example, panoramic photographs are usually 2:1, meaning they are two times wider than they are high.

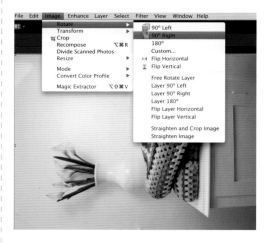

Go to Image > Rotate. Choose which way you want to flip the image. You can also manually rotate an image by clicking on the correct Layer and then Image > Transform > Free Transform. Use the cursor to move the image and click the green tick or press Enter when you're done.

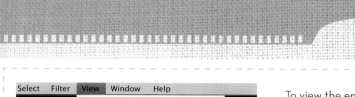

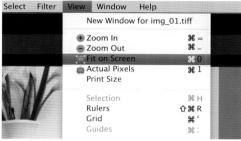

To view the entire image, click View and Fit on Screen.

Click the Straighten button found on the left-hand vertical toolbar. Zoom in on your image by pressing the Z key and clicking on the image. Click over the image and hold to draw a line to demonstrate where the new horizon should be. Release to view the effect.

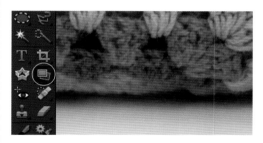

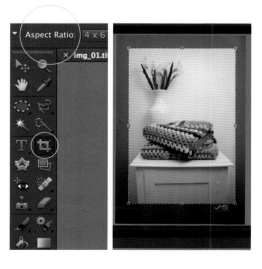

Click the Crop button and click and drag the cursor over the image to make it the size you want. Release the mouse to see a preview and hit Enter to accept the changes. To crop in a particular aspect ratio, use the restraint tool in the top toolbar.

Adjusting Exposure

This is a helpful and important tool when you need to slightly lighten or darken an image to balance the exposure. Exposure is also sometimes called "levels" and "lighting."

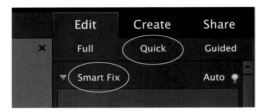

Move from Full to Quick Edit mode. Go to the Lighting section.

Smart Fix is the quickest way to increase lights and darks and balance the midtones. Move the slider to the right until you are satisfied.

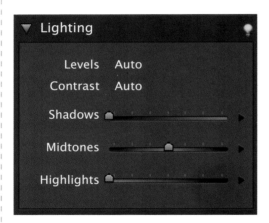

For more control over the changes, move down into the Lighting box. Move the Shadows slider to the right to lighten the dark areas of the image. Move the Highlights slider to the right to darken the light areas of the image. Move the Midtones slider to the right to increase the contrast of everything between black and white. If you're finding it difficult to select the right settings for these three features, you can try clicking Auto Contrast instead.

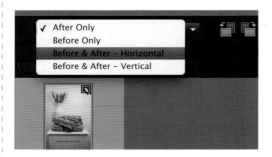

View the Before and After images by clicking the Horizontal option, which can be found above the Project Bin.

If you have adjusted the exposure but aren't sure if you have done too much or too little to improve the image, you can use the histogram as a guide.

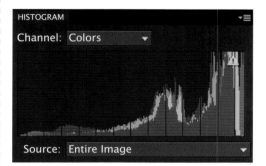

In Full Edit mode, click Window > Histogram. You will notice the histogram appears in the right-hand toolbar. This will give you an idea of the exposure of your image and whether it is too dark or too bright.

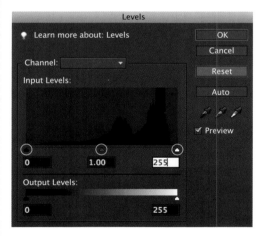

To make more adjustments to the highlights, shadows, and midtones, click Enhance > Adjust Lighting > Levels. Notice the three sliders at the bottom of the graph. Drag the white slider to the left to lighten the highlights, the black slider to the right to darken the shadows, and/or the gray (middle) slider to alter the brightness of the midtones.

Hold down ALT as you adjust highlights and shadows. This turns the image preview to black or white and displays only the areas that have lost some detail or been clipped. Adjust the sliders to lessen or "recover" any clipping.

Correcting Color

Sometimes, even with the best of cameras, lighting, and the most appropriate white-balance setting, colors may still need to be tweaked. To learn more about the concept of color and white balance, refer to page 22.

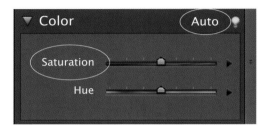

Drop down into the Color section of Quick Edit mode, and click Auto to remove any color-cast. This should make the whites seem whiter. Keep in mind that you may not always need to remove a color-cast, e.g., the warm and flattering glow of a sunset.

BEFORE

AFTER

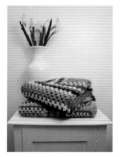 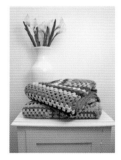

You can also tweak the intensity of color by adjusting the Saturation. Move the Saturation slider to the right to increase the intensity of color, or to the left to decrease it. Hue isn't as relevant, as this slider changes the overall color, and in product photography color should always be accurate.

Be cautious when using tools like saturation, as a little goes a long way. Too much will make an image look unnatural and overprocessed.

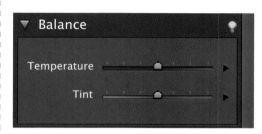

Balance

Temperature

Tint

BEFORE

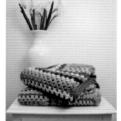

AFTER

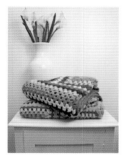

If the colors look almost-but-not-quite right, move down to the Balance section. Slide Temperature to the right to add a warm orange tone to the image or to the left to add more of a cool blue tone. Sliding Tint to the right adds a touch of magenta to the image, and to the left, a touch of green. Your aim should be to make the image look as it did to your eye when you took the photograph. If you're unsure, be gentle and aim for slightly more warm than cool, or skin tone that is ever-so-slightly more magenta than green.

You don't want to spend time correcting the color of an image on your screen, only to find out later on that your monitor wasn't displaying color accurately. Calibrating is a way of checking and changing the color display of your monitor and is an important maintenance tool. There are some free monitor calibration software tools available online, but calibration hardware, such as Datacolor's Spyder3Express, offers a more accurate assessment. Monitor display can change over time, so it's important to calibrate regularly, especially if you work with images on a regular basis.

Optional Extras

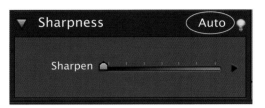

SHARPENING

Sharpening will not recover an out-of-focus image, but it can help to make an in-focus image slightly clearer.

BEFORE

AFTER

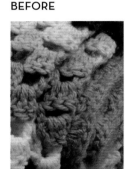

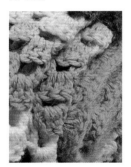

Still in Quick Edit mode, move down to Sharpness. Zoom in to 1:1. This will help you gauge the effect of the sharpening you are about to apply. Click Auto and assess the result. Undo if you are dissatisfied with the effect and slide Sharpen to the right for manual adjustment. Once again, less is more, so be gentle.

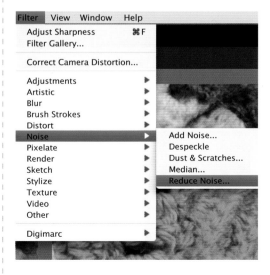

NOISE REDUCTION

Noise reduction can also make an image look clearer. Combining noise reduction and sharpening can be counterproductive, though, as sharpening can, in fact, enhance noise. If you need to add both, apply noise reduction first and then sharpening, and assess the result.

While still zoomed-in, click Filter > Noise > Reduce Noise. The default settings may be acceptable for your image, but if not, return all levels to zero and adjust one by one. Strength affects black-and-white noise, Reduce Color Noise affects color noise, and Preserve Details helps to retain sharpness so that the image does not become too soft or even blurry.

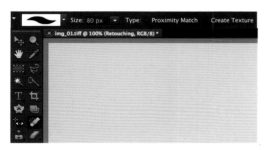

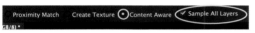

RETOUCHING & REMOVING DUST

Retouching is basically taking a nearby area of the image and blending it over the top of the problem area.

BEFORE

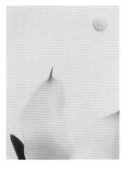

AFTER

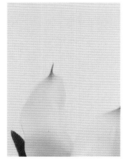

In Full Edit mode, zoom in to 1:1. Click the Spot Healing tool. Increase the size of the tool until it is just slightly bigger than the area you want to retouch. Content-Aware and Sample All Layers should be checked to ensure that the Spot Healing tool looks at the entire image when making these corrections. Click on the affected area and release to see the result. You can also click and drag to remove long/linear blemishes.

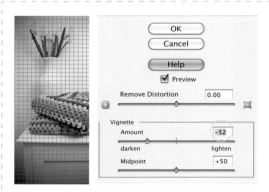

ADDING A VIGNETTE

A vignette will darken the edges of a photograph without affecting the exposure of the center. It's like a graduated border that subtly draws more attention to the center of the photograph.

Go to Filter > Correct Camera Distortion. Slide Vignette Amount to the left to darken (or the right to lighten). If Preview is checked, you will be able to see the effect and adjust accordingly. Click OK when satisfied.

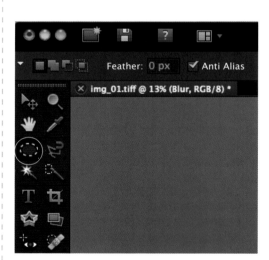

ADDING A DELIBERATE BLUR

An out-of-focus foreground or background is primarily achieved with the lens using its aperture/f-stop settings (pages 16–17). Applying a blur in post-production can have a similar effect.

In Full Edit mode, select the Elliptical Marquee tool from the vertical left-hand toolbar. Make a selection around the object in your image that you would like to keep in focus. It is important to make the selected area quite a bit bigger than your object, as the adjustment process will narrow down the size of your selection.

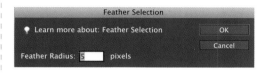

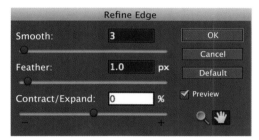

Click Select > Inverse, then Select > Feather. Adjust the value and click OK. The Feather Radius will depend on the overall size of your image and applies the blur adjustment in a graduated way so that you don't have a sharp transition from blur to focus. You may have to experiment to find the right radius to make the transition to blur look right.

Now go to Select > Refine Edge. The important feature here is Contract/Expand and you should use the slider to ensure that most of the area to be blurred is selected and then click OK. Look for the Custom Overlay Color preview feature as this can make it easier to see where the blur will and will not be applied.

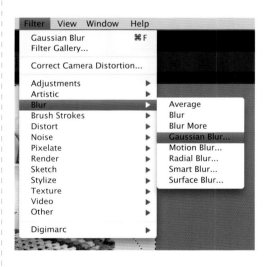

Finally, go to Filter > Blur > Gaussian Blur and adjust the radius until you have the desired effect and click OK. If too much of your image is blurred, start again, but this time select a larger area around the object and lower the Feather Radius value. To view the result, click Select > Deselect.

Digital Files

FILE FORMATS

Digital file formats were developed to package all of the information contained within an image in a useful way. Formats, such as JPEG, TIFF, and PNG, were each designed to meet a particular need, e.g., small file size for online transfer, or high-quality for printing. When an image is saved in any file format, its original details are either entirely preserved, or they are compressed into a smaller version.

CHOOSING THE RIGHT FORMAT

For online display, the priority is usually to keep the file size as low as possible. Suitable image formats would include low- to mid-quality JPEG and PNG. For printing, preserving as much color information as possible is the priority and files like TIFF or high-quality JPEGs would be suitable.

IMAGE COMPRESSION

This occurs when pixels that aren't needed to represent the full image are removed to reduce the file size. There are two types of image compression:

1. Lossless formats, which save files without losing detail. These formats, e.g., TIFF, are suitable for high-quality and professional printing.

2. Lossy formats, which result in lost detail, meaning their overall file size is smaller than lossless formats. These formats are suitable for on-screen display and faster online transfer. However, some formats do still retain enough information to be suitable for printing, such as high-quality JPEG, which is commonly referred to using a scale of 1 to 12, with 1 indicating high-compression and lowest quality, and 12 low-compression and highest quality.

```
Photoshop
Large Document Format
BMP
CompuServe GIF
Dicom
Photoshop EPS
IFF Format
JPEG
JPEG 2000
PCX
Photoshop PDF
Photoshop 2.0
Photoshop Raw
Pixar
PNG
Portable Bit Map
Scitex CT
Targa
✓ TIFF
Photoshop DCS 1.0
Photoshop DCS 2.0
```

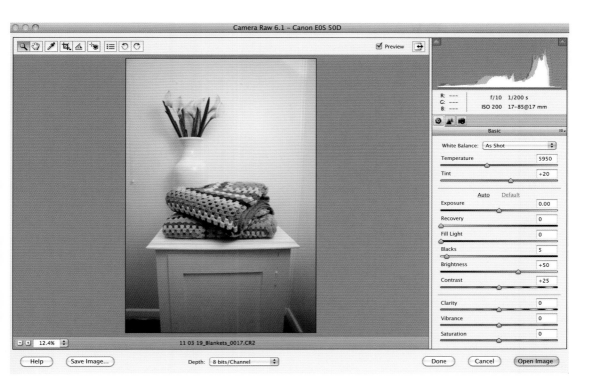

RAW IMAGES

DSLRs and many enthusiasts' compact cameras offer the option of shooting in RAW format. RAW file extensions include CR2 (Canon), NEF (Nikon), SR2 (Sony), and RAF (Fuji). RAW images are saved on the memory card in their original, uncompressed format. This makes the file size larger, so fewer images will fit on a memory card than if you were saving in JPEG.

RAW files give you more flexibility when it comes to editing the image and printing the photograph. For example, Photoshop Elements allows you to complete most common edits in the Camera Raw window, including preset white balance options.

Size & Resolution

The size, or resolution, of an image is simply the number of pixels it contains. Size is the width and height of an image and resolution is the total amount of detail contained within those dimensions. Resolution is often also referred to as the quality of an image. To find the resolution, multiply the width by the height, in pixels. So, an image that is 1800 pixels wide and 1200 pixels high has a resolution of 2,160,000 pixels (also known as 2.16 megapixels/MP). To find the pixel dimensions go to Image > Resize > Image Size.

You may also have seen images referred to as high-resolution and/or low-resolution. This is a general reference to the amount of pixels, or color information, that image contains. There is no minimum or maximum level for low- or high-resolution, as it is dependent on the size of the end-use requirement. Image size is the most useful measure because it is relevant for both on-screen viewing and printing an image.

PRINT RESOLUTION

This is an instruction given to a printer about how many pixels from an image to print in every inch of the final photograph. This is referred to as pixels per inch or ppi (and sometimes also incorrectly referred to as dots per inch [dpi]—ppi is more accurate). It is generally accepted that 300ppi (and higher) will result in a high-quality print and under 150ppi in a low-quality print. It is difficult, however, to see the improvement in print quality beyond 300ppi.

PRINT SIZE

To find the maximum print size of an image, use this simple equation:
width or height (in pixels) ÷ ppi = print size in inches

For example:
(1800 ÷ 300) × (1200 ÷ 300) pixels = 6in × 4in

Image size remains the same (unless you crop the image down to a smaller size) and so it is the print resolution that determines the final printed size. Lowering print resolution is a way to increase the size at which your image can be printed. For example, if you drop the resolution to between 150 and 299ppi, you will print a larger-sized photograph, but you may also see some loss of quality. This is because you are using fewer pixels and, thus, less information to fill each inch of the image.

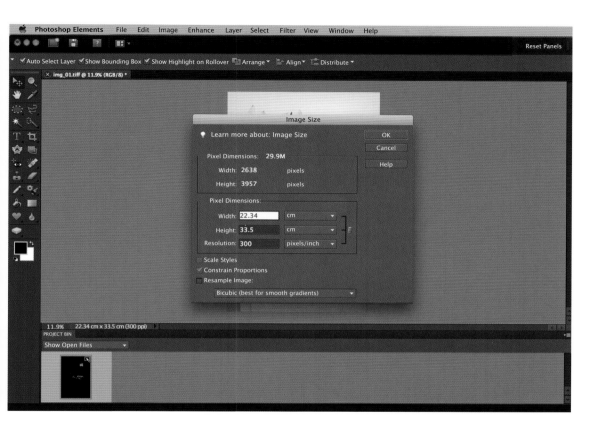

RESOLUTION & YOUR CAMERA

Every digital camera has a maximum width and height at which it can produce an image at full size. This is directly related to the size of the camera's sensor and is often expressed as a total number of megapixels. Check your camera's manual for the maximum image size it supports.

If you've been told that your images are unsuitable for use in the press, it is usually because your images are too small or low quality. Your camera may be set to take images on a low-quality setting or it may not have a large enough sensor to take high-quality large-size images. This is one reason why many professional photographers use DSLR cameras with very good sensors; their images will be large in size and resolution, allowing them to print large, high-quality photographs.

Protection

The copyright of a photograph is the exclusive legal right to print and reproduce the image. It is held by the creator of the photograph, unless they sell it to a third party or if the photographer is acting on behalf of their employer, which is work for hire. Preserving copyright is important because it encourages creativity by rewarding artists and inventors for original work. When people copy other artists' photographs, use them without permission or use them as their own, they are breaking the law. In addition to holding the copyright, there are a few things you can do to your digital files to try to further protect them.

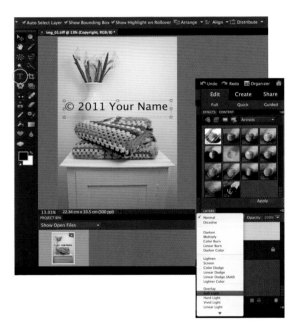

ADDING A WATERMARK

Watermarks are simply semitransparent badges made from text or graphics that are pasted over the top of the image (very similar to an artist's signature on a painting). There are a few things to consider before adding a watermark:

→ They can often easily be removed using software, so they don't guarantee protection against misuse and infringement of copyright.

→ Large, bold, or obvious watermarks can distract your viewer and prevent them from appreciating your photograph in its entirety.

→ You need to be able to reproduce the image without the watermark. Otherwise, if the media or other body requests to use or purchase your image, it will probably be rejected.

Use the Type Tool to add a layer of text to your image. Soften the text using Blending Mode.

UPLOADING SMALL VERSIONS

Quality reproduction of your photographs requires that they contain plenty of pixels, and/or that they are large in size. Small-size, low-resolution images work perfectly well for online display. So, by restricting the width and height of your online photographs, copycats will struggle to make a high-quality reproduction.

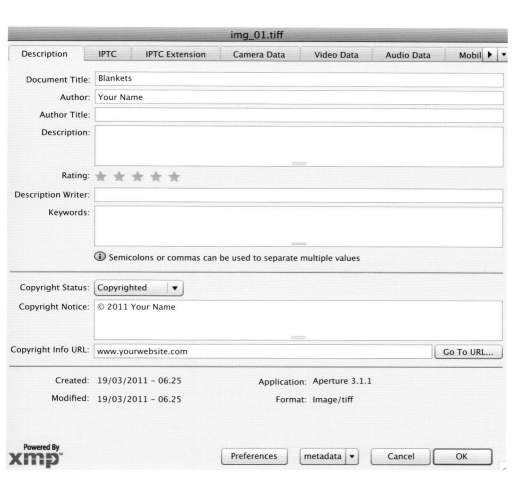

INCLUDING METADATA

Metadata is information taken from the camera and stored in the digital image. Metadata is only visible when viewed using computer software, so it is a less conspicuous way of adding more protection to your images than using a watermark. Similar to watermarks, however, metadata will not completely protect your image from infringement of copyright or misuse, as it can also be digitally removed or "stripped" from an image. Metadata can include the following:

→ Camera make and model, and settings such as exposure, focal length, and applied edits.
→ Date and time the image was taken.
→ Copyright information, including your name, address, and website.

Take a look at the dialog box that opens under File > File Info > Description.

Saving & Storing

Saving, or exporting, an image simply involves taking it from the photo-editing software, along with any edits you have applied, creating a copy and saving it somewhere, like in a folder or attached to an email. It is during this stage that you can export the file in its original size or specify the width, height, and print-resolution values of the image. For example, in Photoshop Elements, move to the Share tab and click Email Attachments. This will prompt you to save a copy of the file and then open the Organizer Workspace, where you can click and drag the image(s) into the box provided and specify the file-size details.

NAMING IMAGES

Getting into the habit of renaming images when you save or export them will make them much easier to find in future. Your options for naming images are countless, but some suggestions are:
→ YearMonthProjectCount.jpg
   (e.g., 1109Crochet01.jpg)
→ ProjectTypeCount.jpg
   (e.g., CrochetBlanket01.jpg)
→ TypeYearMonthCount.jpg
   (e.g., Blanket110901.jpg)

STORING IMAGES

You need to keep your images safe but also accessible. Create a series of clear and meaningful folders in which to store your images. Once again, you have plenty of pathway options, such as:
→ Year > Month > Project > Type
   e.g., 2011 > 09 > Crochet > Blanket
→ Project > Type > Year > Month
   e.g., Crochet > Blanket > 2011 > 09
→ Client > Year > Month > Project > Type e.g.,
   Handmade Fair > 2011 > 09 > Crochet > Blanket

If you have thousands of images scattered all around your computer in no logical order, prioritize time to whip them back into shape. This task is time-consuming and not at all interesting, but it's a time-saver in the long run.

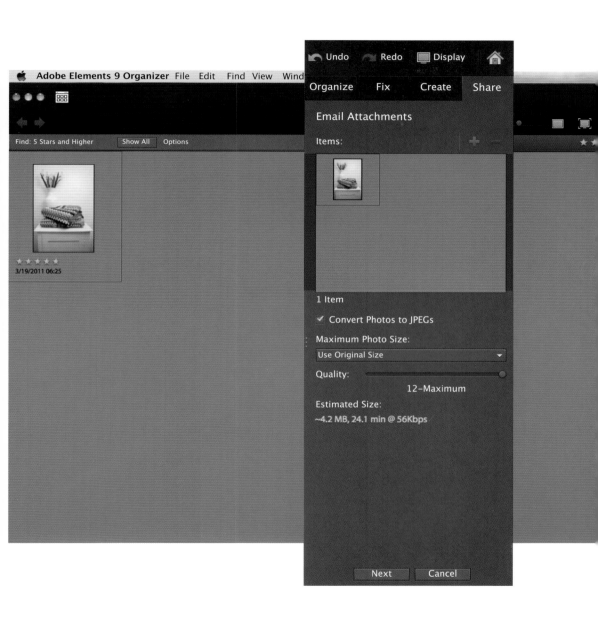

Backing Up

Sadly, it's often the case that people who are the most committed to backing up their images are the ones who have lost them all before. If you aren't one of these people, you're lucky. You can take this opportunity to take steps to prevent losing everything on your computer. Frustratingly, no method of backup offers an absolute guarantee of safety and security. What is guaranteed, though, is that choosing not to back up gives you practically no chance at all of recovering important files after they have been lost.

To back up your images, you need to store a copy of the original and edited files on a device that is separate from your computer, ideally also in an off-site location. The process is simple, but the practicalities can become tedious, so it's best to make backing up part of your routine, whether you like it or not.

EXTERNAL MEMORY DEVICES

An external drive is a device that contains memory. Examples include portable hard drives or USB thumb or flash drives. External drives are good investments: they're affordable, widely available, small, lightweight, can be stored off-site, and you can select one with as much or as little capacity as you need.

CDS AND DVDS

Storing images on disc is a cheap and easy way to back up. Keep in mind, however, that they do degrade over time and can still easily be damaged, lost, or stolen.

DEDICATED EXTERNAL BACKUP HARDWARE AND SOFTWARE

If you deal with a seriously large amount of images, you should consider investing in a dedicated, external, backup device. These usually work by taking a copy of the full contents of your computer and then tracking any changes that are made from that date forward. Software then allows you to access those copied files at any stage. An example is Apple's Time Capsule (hardware) and Time Machine (software).

THE CLOUD

Cloud computing is the term used to describe the sharing of resources on the Internet. Storing a copy of your images in "The Cloud" on websites such as www.dropbox.com is a simple and easy way of creating a secure off-site backup. You can create a private account that links your computer, phone, and laptop and is accessible using an Internet connection from anywhere in the world.

Other photo-management websites, including www.flickr.com, offer space to upload images that you can also keep private. When you upgrade to a Pro account on Flickr, you can upload (and download) an original image as long as each file is 20MB or under.

[1] Hand-Crocheted Hooded Cowl
Nikon D80
1/65 sec, f/4.8, ISO 200, 48mm
Hurley Sashimi

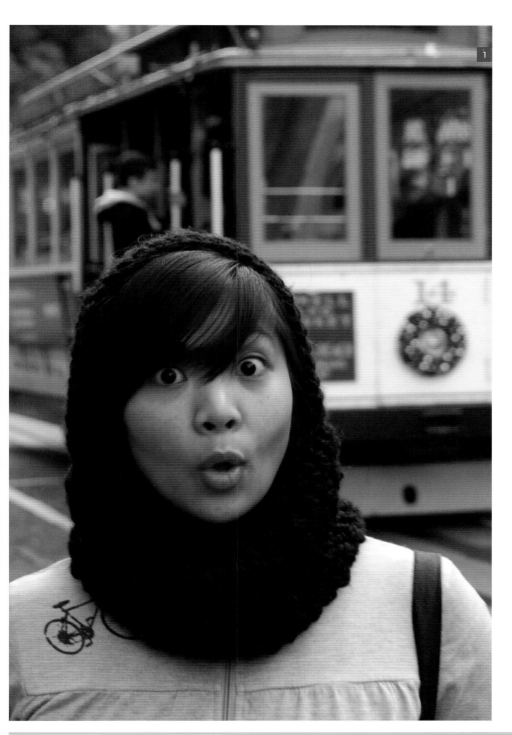

Camera Workflow

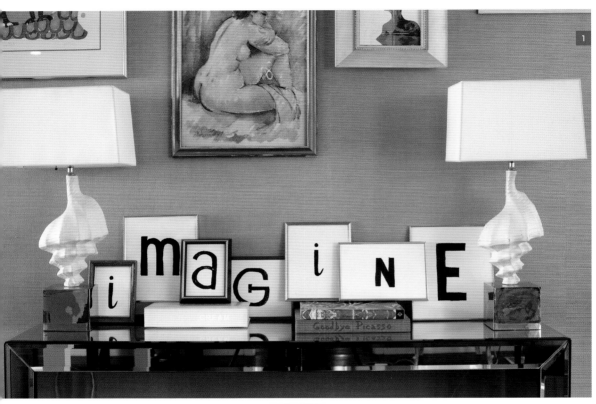

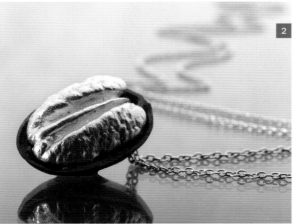

[1] Imagine
Canon EOS 5D
1/8 sec, f/5.6, ISO 500, 50mm
Gayle Brooker

[2] Silver Pecan Necklace
Aptus 22
1/125 sec, f/2.3, ISO 100, 120mm
Roee Raifeld

Every camera is different and you need to find what works best for you. In the meantime, here is a suggested workflow:

1. **Camera Maintenance**
   Store the camera in a dry, cool, and secure place. Clean and protect the lens.

2. **Planning and Setup**
   Clean/tidy your product(s) and setting. Prepare your background, props, and styling, and position your product(s).

3. **Two Charged Batteries**
   Always start with a fully charged battery in the camera with another on standby.

4. **Two Empty Memory Cards**
   Ensure that the images from your last shoot have all been downloaded and securely backed up. Then, format your card between uses. Have one spare card for the shoot.

5. **Camera Modes and Options**
   Select your desired mode, e.g., Macro or Av. Set other relevant options, e.g., continuous shooting and the central focal point.

6. **Image Format and Quality**
   Set this to the highest level available, e.g. RAW or X-Large JPEG.

7. **White Balance**
   Choose the white balance that best suits your shooting environment, or AUTO if you're unsure.

8. **Take a Light-Meter Reading**
   If your camera allows, look through the viewfinder and press the shutter release halfway. Adjust exposure settings accordingly.

9. **Set the ISO/ASA Level**
   The default will usually be AUTO or your previously used setting. Moving away from AUTO will help you achieve the desired exposure, and using a low ISO will result in minimal noise/grain.

10. **Shutter and Aperture**
    Adjust accordingly, if applicable.

11. **Exposure Compensation**
    Adjust accordingly, if applicable.

12. **Compose the Scene**
    Adjust your shooting position, angle, and the focal length by zooming in or out.

13. **Take and Preview the Photograph**
    Hold steady or use a tripod. If possible, halfway press the shutter to prefocus the lens before releasing the shutter.

14. **Adjust the Exposure and/or Scene**
    If necessary, adjust the aperture, shutter, and/or ISO to improve the exposure, and move your products, styling, or background, and recompose. Take another photograph and compare with the last. Continue with steps 13 and 14 until complete.

15. **Download/Import and Back Up**
    Copy images from your camera to your computer and back up as soon as possible.

Post-production Workflow

A good workflow allows you to take the least amount of time to achieve the best result. There is no right or wrong method, so, again, find what works for you. In the meantime, here is an example:

1. **Selecting**
   Browse through the imported images and rate any that you think are acceptable with the number one or one star. When you're done with the first pass, go through again, this time increasing your rating to two, as you look for the better images out of the acceptable bunch. Repeat until you have found the good-from-better, and best-from-good images. Don't take too much time on the first and second pass, and don't be afraid to leave out any images that you're unsure of—you don't want to waste time editing images that you won't use, and you can always go back to the lower-rated images later on.

2. **Create a Duplicate Layer**
   If your software does not offer a Duplicate Layer option, ensure that you have your original files backed up so that you can revert to them should you permanently save any unwanted edits on an image.

3. **Rotate, Straighten, and Crop**
   If you need to change the aspect ratio, remove a distraction, rotate, or straighten, do so now.

4. **Adjust Exposure**
   Take a look at the histogram to check the exposure. Adjust highlights, shadows, and midtones up or down accordingly.

5. **Color Correction**
   Check the white balance and adjust accordingly.

6. **Retouch/Remove Dust**
   Zoom in on the affected area to do any retouching.

7. **Other Edits**
   Now is the time to add in any other edits that you think may improve your photograph, such as noise reduction or sharpening.

8. **Export/Save**
   Meaningfully name the file, select a logical storage pathway, set the appropriate size and print resolution. You may wish to include a watermark or a selection of metadata in your export.

9. **File Check**
   Take a quick look inside the folder you have chosen/created, to ensure that the file(s) have exported correctly and the images are displaying properly.

10. **Back up**
    Save a copy of your original files and the edited versions on your backup device. Store your backup device carefully and securely.

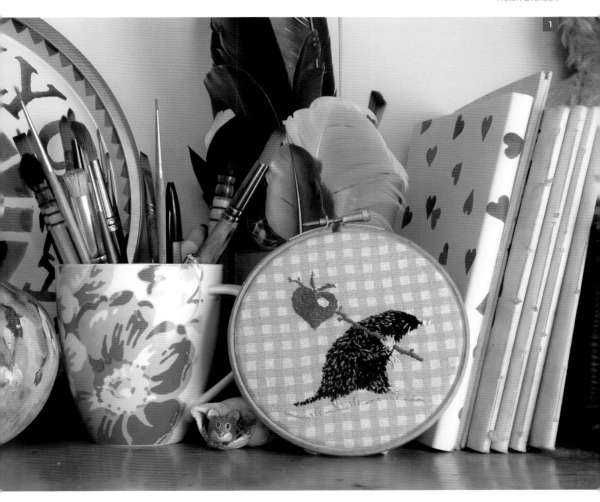

Troubleshooting

The photographs below show two examples where the lighting, styling, and composition have deliberately been kept simple so that they don't compete with the product for attention. Compare these with the 16 others on the right that show examples of common problems.

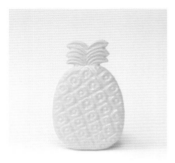 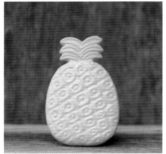

Yellow Pineapple Brooch
Canon EOS 50D
1/320 sec, f/2, ISO 100, 50mm
Heidi Adnum

1. **Problem:** Underexposed
   Fix: Use larger aperture/slower shutter/higher ISO/increase exposure compensation/increase lighting. See pages 10–21.

2. **Problem:** Overexposed
   Fix: Use smaller aperture/faster shutter/lower ISO/decrease exposure compensation/decrease lighting. See pages 10–21.

3. **Problem:** Hard light
   Fix: Soften the light. See pages 10–15.

4. **Problem:** Out of focus
   Fix: Stabilize yourself and/or the camera. Use prefocus and/or faster shutter. See pages 24–25.

5. **Problem:** Product is sideways
   Fix: Rotate image. See pages 144–145.

6. **Problem:** Awkward product position
   Fix: Straighten the horizon. See pages 144–145.

7. **Problem:** Product too small in frame
   Fix: Recompose to get closer to the product/ crop in post-production. See pages 38–41 and pages 144–145.

8. **Problem:** Distracting shadow
   Fix: Recompose to get closer to the product/ crop in post-production. See pages 38–41 and pages 144–145.

9. **Problem:** Unflattering angle
   Fix: Shoot from a less severe angle or straight on. See pages 38–41.

10. **Problem:** Distracting background
    Fix: Select a more suitable background. See pages 42–47.

11. **Problem:** Uncomplementary background
    Fix: Select a more suitable background. See pages 42–47.

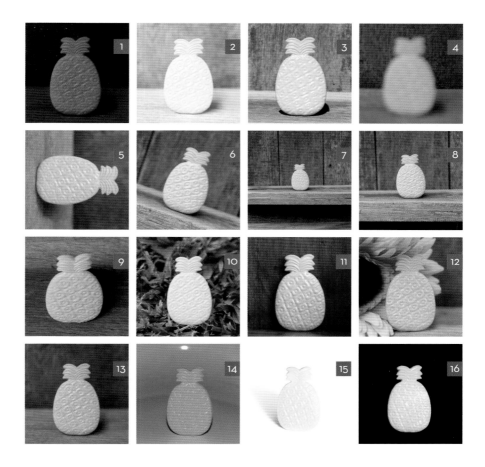

12. **Problem:** Irrelevant, inappropriate prop
    Fix: Remove prop/select a better prop.
    See pages 48–51.

13. **Problem:** Inaccurate color
    Fix: Check exposure/set correct white balance
    on-camera/adjust white balance in post-
    production. See pages 20–23 and pages 148–149.

14. **Problem:** Shiny background, reflected flash,
    glare, lacks depth
    Fix: Select a subtle background/move away
    from full-automatic mode and on-camera flash by
    learning about light and how to make better use
    of the camera. See pages 10–15 and pages 32–35.

15. **Problem:** High contrast white, orange/pink
    shadows, detail lost around edges of product
    Fix: Select a softer light and a more subtle
    background/use a white seamless background/
    less post-production. See pages 10–15 and
    pages 42–47.

16. **Problem:** High-contrast black, product is over-
    powered and appears to be floating,
    lacks depth
    Fix: Select a softer, less harsh, more natural
    background/less post-production. See pages
    42–47 and pages 166–167.

End Uses

How you intend to use your product photographs can determine how you plan and style them, in addition to how you prepare and export the files.

ONLINE SHOPS & MARKETPLACES

Consider the aspect ratio, image size, and overall file size of your image. Normally, the host website will provide information on their requirements, e.g., www.bigcartel.com presently specifies that each image file should be 1000 x 1000 pixels and under 1MB. Select these options—1:1 crop restraint and maximum size 1000px—during the edit and export stage, and the host website will not have to resize your images, which will appear on-screen as you planned. If you have done this and your file size is still too large, apply more compression by re-exporting at a lower quality, e.g., from 12 to 10 on the JPEG quality scale, and so on.

BLOGS, BOOKS & EDITORIAL FEATURES

Media will usually require a photograph of your product either in situ (they may also refer to this as a lifestyle image), or against a plain white background, or both. Editors and authors may request large, high-quality files for print, too.

MARKETING & MERCHANDISING

Here, it's helpful to photograph other elements of your product, such as its packaging, labels, and tags, and showcase your range and coordinating pieces. See page 48 for more.

COMPETITIONS

Requirements for competitions vary. Sometimes they are the same as for online shops, and other times they are more involved—it will depend on the individual competition. If required to show the functionality of your product, in situ styling would be perfect. If asked to show the product alone and without any distractions, use a seamless, neutral background. Competitions can also specify a minimum/maximum file size, and they may also only accept images with minimal editing.

YOUR CUSTOMERS

Whether your product reaches your customers through your online shop, a marketing campaign, a blog, or a book, they are your ultimate end users. Customers are what really counts, as they pay for your product, incorporate it into their lives, and, if satisfied, tell their friends about it. Customers want to be seduced by great photographs that show a product's design, features, and functionality.

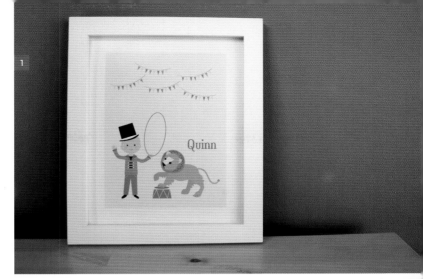

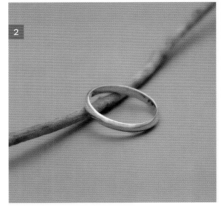

[1] Olliegraphic Name Print
Minolta DiMAGE Z1
1/100 sec, f/4.5, ISO 50, 9.7mm
Meg Bartholomy

[2] Smiley Ring
Nikon D70
1/125 sec, f/4.5, ISO 200, 70mm
Tooli's Jewelry

[3] Linen Fabric Art Doll
Konica Minolta DiMAGE A2
1/200 sec, f/3.5, ISO 100, 49mm
Izabela Nikiel

[4] Liberty Print Tova Top
Nikon D80
1/80 sec, f/4.5, ISO 640, 50mm
Jenny Gordy

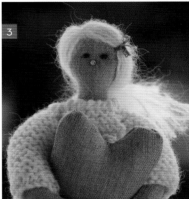

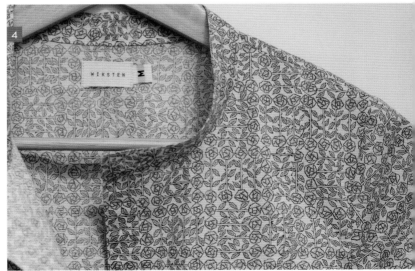

Branding, Marketing & Merchandising

Consistently and gracefully executed branding, marketing, and merchandising allows small businesses to begin competing with larger companies, even with a low budget. Your strategies should always be goal-oriented, and your objectives should be specific, measurable, achievable, realistic, and time-bound (SMART).

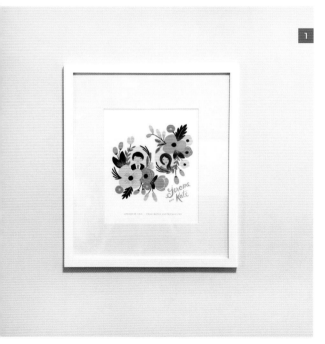

BRANDING

Developing a brand helps your business and products to stand out by giving them an identity. Your brand is made up of everything that people associate with your business, product, service, and you. Notice that successful brands are consistent, relevant, and they always stand out. But they also know exactly what they do and how they do it better than anyone else.

MARKETING

An effective marketing strategy communicates with customers how a product will meet their needs. This makes the product desirable and appealing to the customer and will attract them to your shop. Developing your marketing strategy should involve honest analysis of your strengths, weaknesses, opportunities, and threats. This "SWOT" analysis is a great way to really understand your product and its features from a customer's point of view, what sets your brand apart from your competitors, your target market, and business environment.

[1] Custom Illustrated Portrait Print
Nikon D80
1/5 sec, f/4.8, ISO 200, 44mm
Rifle Paper Co.

[2] Assorted Hat Card Set
Nikon D80
1/125 sec, f/4.2, ISO 400, 32mm
Rifle Paper Co.

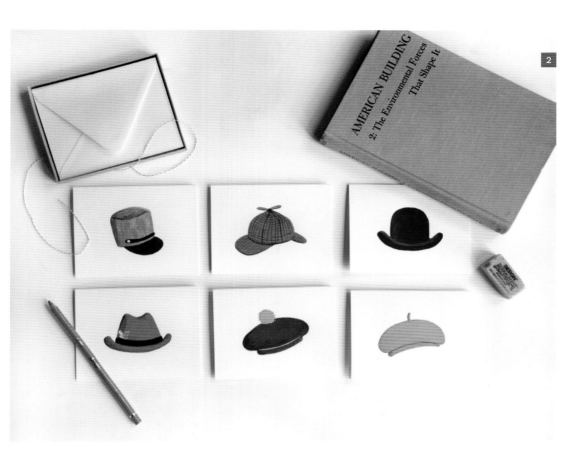

MERCHANDISING

Merchandising is all about planning, organizing, and promoting your product to the right people at the right time. Good merchandising makes the customer want to get close to your product, to touch it, and to imagine how it may impact upon their lives. Good online merchandising helps to make the customer feel more comfortable that they are making the right decision to purchase a product that they have only ever seen in photographs.

Good Business Practice

It is good business practice to have a set of guidelines for optimal performance and to help you achieve your goals. Consider the following:

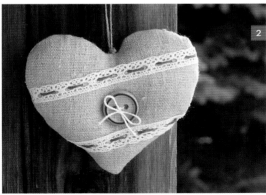

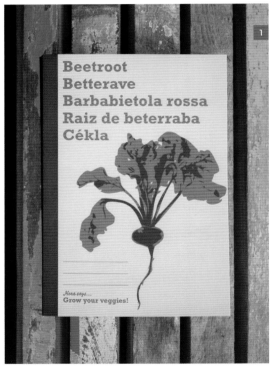

YOUR PRODUCT AND SERVICE

→ Be a specialist, know your niche or point-of-difference from competitors.

→ Create desire among customers, making them want to own a part of your brand.

→ Offer excellent customer service to make customers feel fabulous and comfortable with your brand.

→ Add value by being courteous, polite, and purposeful, and pay close attention to customers' needs.

→ Become aware of any product or service weaknesses, and commit to strengthening them, if possible.

→ Be serious about strict quality assurance, including thorough and accurate product descriptions.

YOUR BUSINESS

→ Set goals to achieve and sustain growth, including profit-and-loss analysis.

→ Minimize waste, nurture employees, and best-use other resources.

→ Continue learning and improving through regular training and customer feedback.

→ Create an efficient and meaningful record-keeping system.

→ Carry out regular system maintenance and back up, including up-to-date warranties and insurance, and a contingency plan, should ever you need it.

→ Understand your own values, such as fairness, ethics, and work–life balance.

[1] **Nora Whynot Beetroot Garden Journal**
Canon Rebel XSi
1/125 sec, f/4.5, ISO 200, 50mm
Nora Whynot

[2] **Linen Heart Ornament**
Konica Minolta DiMAGE A2
1/80 sec, f/4.5, ISO 100, 18mm
Izabela Nikiel

[3] **Nora Whynot Ruler Exercise Books**
Canon Rebel XSi
1/100 sec, f/4.5, ISO 200, 50mm
Nora Whynot

THE ROLE OF YOUR PHOTOGRAPHS

Great product photography can be used to send the right messages to your customers and is especially important if your business is largely or entirely online. Consistently styled and composed photos help to build your brand. They can also save you money: Select your best photos, which sum up your shop, and use them for such things as your:
→ logo, avatar, banner, and signage;
→ tags, labels, and business cards;
→ website design;
→ advertisements, giveaways, and promotions; and
→ how-to guides.

They also contribute to merchandising, which is difficult without a physical setup to guide customers around displays, and to touch and feel your product. Examples include:
→ Grouping products—whether part of a set or complementary designs. This suggests to your customer ways in which they might use your product and which ones match. It's similar to the "Customers also bought" and "You may also be interested in" feature on many popular websites.

→ In-situ styling—this encourages your customers to imagine your product in use and how that might make them feel.

YOUR ROLE

Great photographs are critical for online business success, but you know that they alone aren't enough. Learn from reputable organizations and industry experts that publish information on business development and improvement. A low budget can be restrictive, but don't let it stop you: A confident, professional attitude, fine attention to detail, dedication, and personalized service cost nothing; nor does the annual review of your programs and systems. Most importantly, understand your own value as a company resource. Know your product better than anyone else. Understand the needs of your customers and the state of the market. Convey your passion and enthusiasm for your product and service to make your customers feel great and delight in the experience of buying from you. Customer loyalty is earned and can be one of your strongest assets.

Social Networking

Social networks offer you the opportunity to market your product and business, connect with your customers, receive feedback in real time, carry out market research, and showcase your beautiful photography, all of which, ideally, will lead to more interest in your product. These websites are usually free and easy to use, and can be a great tool for word-of-mouth advertising. They can make customers feel closer to you and your business and can act as vehicles to motivate others to share information about your products and ethos. For all of these reasons, being a part of a social network is a good idea.

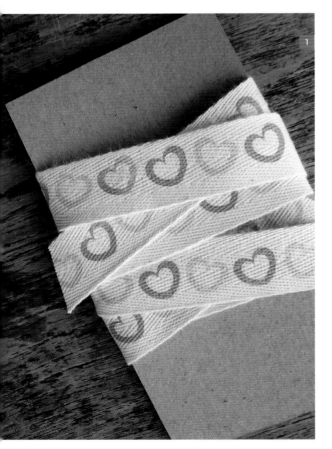

Given all the options, though, it is understandable to feel a little overwhelmed and confused about the right social networks to choose. The decision of whether to join at all, or which one(s), is entirely up to you and what best suits your style and your goals.

Many social networking websites also offer paid advertising, which can allow you to reach a more targeted market. However, if your budget is very small, you don't have to pay for advertising for your efforts to be effective: Simply having an online presence and interacting with your customers in a meaningful and unique way will help to grow your brand. For paid advertising at a more affordable price, look to relevant, successful blogs, as they will probably offer advertising slots priced with small businesses in mind. Handmade marketplaces, such as www.poppytalkhandmade.com and www.papernstitch.com, are also great ways of showcasing your product for a reasonable fee to viewers who you know have an interest in handmade products.

Be sure to balance your time spent online with learning and support. Online business resources, such as www.designspongeonline.com Biz Lady series, can offer excellent—and free—advice.

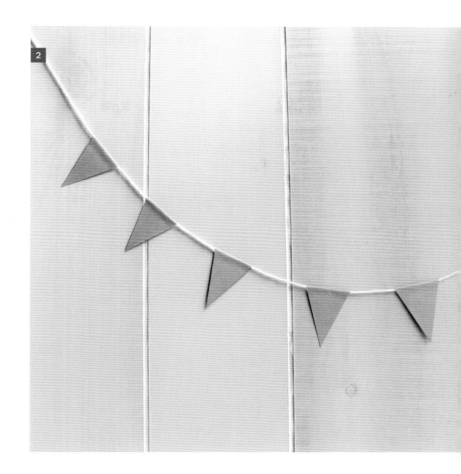

[1] Hand-printed Ribbon
Kodak DX7590
1/100 sec, f/2.8, ISO 80, 6.3mm
Alarna Zinn

[2] Bunting Stickers
Canon PowerShot S2 IS
1/80 sec, f/2.7, ISO 200, 6mm
Natalie Jost

Networks such as *www.facebook.com*, *www.twitter.com*, and blogs such as *www.blogger.com* and *www.wordpress.com*, are great platforms for building customer relationships and sharing information with your customers about new products, discounts, and deals.

Photo-sharing websites like *www.flickr.com* and blogs are great for creating an extensive collection of your photographs.

Pin-boards like *www.pinterest.com* are great places to share more of your personality, taste, or style by building lists of favorite photographs—mainly those created by other people.

Finding Motivation

When it's all going well, photography can be a load of fun, but like any other business essential, photography can also be an involved, complex, and frustrating process. During these times, it can be very hard to find the motivation to continue. The good news is that product photography will become much more gratifying when you have a better understanding of light and your camera.

Practice is essential, regardless of your experience level, and it is normal to have bad days and make mistakes. Don't be afraid or ashamed to ask for help if you need it—consider taking a course, whether free or paid-for, face-to-face, or online. Many professionals take annual refresher courses for continued learning and growth.

As your understanding of light and photography develops, you may outgrow your camera. This is normal and a sure sign that your photographic skills and photographs are better than ever. If you need better equipment, consider buying it a worthwhile investment in the success and development of your business.

Upgrading doesn't have to mean expensive equipment, as this doesn't automatically make anyone a good photographer. If you're not ready to upgrade, commit to making the most of the equipment and surroundings you have available to you right now and you will almost certainly become a better photographer.

To make shoots more enjoyable, listen to your favorite music and keep up your energy levels with plenty of delicious snacks and water. Enlist help from your biggest fans, even if it's just to bring snacks or chat with you during the shoot. Know that professional shoots can also be hot and stuffy, time-consuming, frustrating, and still turn out quite a few bad photographs—you just don't get to see them!

Keep thinking about what photographs you like and continue to practice, especially with the subjects you love—this is the way to develop your own style. If you're still feeling stuck, take time to nurture yourself and your creativity. Take a break and go to the places that inspire and relax you. This will help you to come up with ideas for photographs or generate energy and motivation for your next shoot.

Whatever you do, though, don't give up.

[1] Batman and Robin Print
Canon PowerShot SX110 IS
1/125 sec, f/2.8, ISO 400, 78mm
Judy Kaufmann

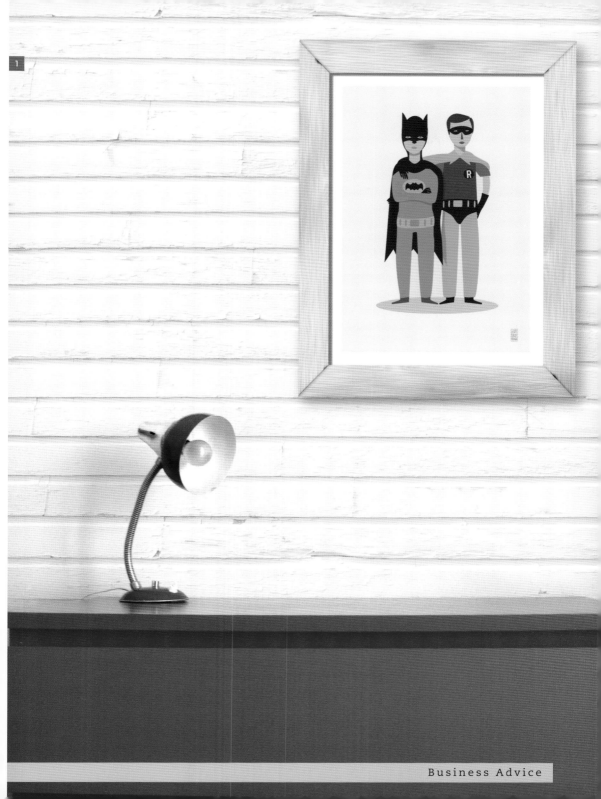

Practitioner Spotlight
Re Jin Lee

How do you take photographs that show off your products so beautifully?

I prefer to use a white background to photograph my products and shoot them in daylight. The images come out clean and the details of my products stand out. Most importantly, all the images look cohesive when grouped together.

What has been the best photography-related lesson or tip you have received?

Back up your files!

What do you know now that would have made photographing your products and dealing with digital images easier for you in the beginning?

I wish I hadn't been as intimidated as I was with manual settings when I first started shooting. If I had taken the time to learn, instead of relying on the full-automatic setting, I would've spent less time using editing software and would have a quality archive of photographs of my first products.

What do you think are common mistakes people make when it comes to photographing handcrafted items?

All I can say is that my most common mistake is that I don't use a tripod as often as I should for stability. The image might look good on camera, but it doesn't look as good on the screen at full size.

What advice do you have for other crafters who are looking for excellent photographs of their products at home or on a budget?

Create a seamless white background using a table against a wall near a window with smooth, white paper and tape. If the weather is gloomy, use a clamp-light or two, with daylight bulbs to help out. Lastly, use a tripod!

When photographing your products, are you thinking about your brand, promotion, and possible end uses?

I keep all the end uses in mind, such as my websites, press kits, printed linesheets, and postcards. For example, when I can only show one image per product, I shoot one frame, where the most important feature of the product is clear. Or, for online shoppers, I want to make sure they get to see every important detail of the product, so I use the macro lens to get in close and capture the details.

How has social networking helped to develop your business?

My photographs received great exposure on social networking websites and that has led to many blog features and word-of-mouth interest in my products.

Can you share any advice on how to improve a business model?

You're more inclined to have a successful day if you set your work hours and fill them productively and have a to-do list. Set a shoot date and hours, prepare a list or a reference board for lighting, composition, colors, etc., and shoot away.

Shop name
Bailey Doesn't Bark

Website
www.baileydoesntbark.com

Make and model of camera
Canon PowerShot G10 and Canon
EOS 5D

Most used camera settings
RAW, 1/30 sec, f/2.8, 24mm

**Most used camera/lighting
accessories**
Tripod

Favorite time of day to shoot
9am–11am

Favorite location
Still-life table near a window

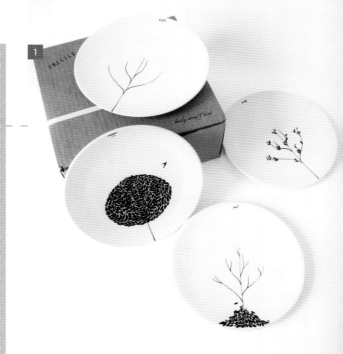

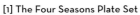

[1] The Four Seasons Plate Set
Canon PowerShot G10
1/40 sec, f/2.8, ISO 200, 24mm

[2] Floresta Bowl No. 8
Canon PowerShot G10
1/40 sec, f/2.8, ISO 200, 24mm

All products manufactured and
photographed by *Bailey Doesn't Bark*

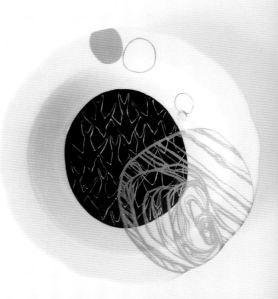

Glossary

aperture
The opening of a lens that allows in light to create an exposure on the camera's sensor.

aspect ratio
The ratio of the width of an image to its height.

backlight
Also called a Rim Light; a light source that falls on the object from behind.

bulb exposure
A camera mode that keeps the shutter open for as long as the shutter-release is pressed.

center of interest
A rule of photographic composition that suggests a photograph should have only one main idea or focal point.

color depth
The number of bits used to represent the color of each pixel. Typical values are 8, 16, and 24 (true color).

color profile
Information that defines a color space. Used in computer and printer software to ensure colors are reproduced accurately. Generic CMYK and sRGB are examples.

depth of field
The distance between the nearest and farthest objects in focus in a photograph.

Drive Mode
Also called Burst or Continuous Mode, this enables the shutter to operate multiple times in a single press of the shutter-release.

exposure
The amount of light received by the sensor of a camera via the lens.

exposure compensation
A feature that overrides automatic or semi-automatic exposure settings by forcing the camera to over- or under-expose an image, usually by adjusting the shutter or aperture.

focal length
The distance between the camera's sensor and the center of the lens.

focus
A clear and sharp image that is achieved by adjusting the lens.

film speed
A system developed to measure the sensitivity to light of photographic film or the digital sensor equivalent, often referred to as the ISO or ASA level.

f-stop
A measure of lens aperture, calculated by dividing aperture diameter with focal length.

histogram
A graph that shows the distribution of shadows, midtones, and highlights of an image. The horizontal axis represents white, black, and color, and the vertical axis shows the number of pixels represented by that color.

image compression
A process designed to make a digital image smaller in size and easier to handle, store, email, and post online.

ISO
From the International Standards Organization and relates to the speed/sensitivity of film. The ISO setting on a digital camera is a calculation of its film equivalent.

key light
The main light a photographer uses to illuminate a scene.

kicker light
A light that is used to control shadows and highlights; usually not the main source of light.

leading lines
A rule of photographic composition that suggests lines can lead into and out of an image, attracting the eye and leading it through the photograph.

light meter
Also known as an Exposure Meter. A light-sensitive device built in to digital cameras that measures reflected light and is used to determine exposure.

megapixel
The standard way to measure the resolution of a digital camera and is equivalent to one million pixels.

noise
Unwanted artifacts in a photograph, such as small dots of color that are more likely to occur as the ISO level increases.

pixel
An abbreviation of Picture Element. Each pixel is a tiny dot of color determined by the intensity of light.

rule of thirds
A rule of photographic composition that suggests the point of interest in a photograph should be placed in one of four places found by dividing the photograph into thirds and using one point at which a vertical and horizontal line meet.

sensor
The light-sensitive part of a camera that receives light from the lens and turns it into an image, either digital or analog (film).

shutter
A mechanical cover that opens and closes to allow in light to a camera via the lens for a defined period of time.

SLR camera
Single Lens Reflex cameras use a mirror to reflect light from a lens to the viewfinder, allowing the photographer to see directly through the lens. The mirror moves out of the way when the shutter is pressed.

white balance
Accurate display of white in an image, resulting in the correct display of all other colors.

Photographers' Details

Arranged alphabetically according to surname if individual name and first word if company name

Heidi Adnum
www.heidiadnum.com

Galaxie Andrews
www.galaxieandrews.com

Mary Andrews
www.contrary.etsy.com

Jennifer Arndt
www.jenniferarndt.etsy.com

Bailey Doesn't Bark
www.baileydoesntbark.com

Meg Bartholomy
www.olliegraphic.com

Marie Bee
www.marie-bee.com

Bespoke Letterpress
www.bespokeletterpress.com.au

John Birdsong
www.johnbirdsong.etsy.com

Celia Boaz
www.glitzglitter.etsy.com

Stacey Bradley
www.perlaanne.etsy.com

Bill Bradshaw
www.billbradshaw.co.uk

Gayle Brooker
www.gaylebrooker.com

Lisa Bruemmer
www.treeandkimball.etsy.com

Elizabeth Bryant
www.grayworksdesign.etsy.com

Emma Burcusel
www.emmaburcusel.com

Alicia Carrier
www.alice.carbonmade.com

Michelle Chang
www.michellechang.com

Pei Li Chin
www.peiliminiatures.com

Rodica Cioplea
www.rodi-art.com

Samantha Cotterill
www.mummysam.com

Olga Courtnage
www.knittles.ca

Hagar Cygler
www.hagar-studio.tumblr.com

Darlingtonia Moccasin Company
www.darlingtoniamoccasins.com

Helen Dickson
www.bustleandsew.blogspot.com

William Dohman
www.ohdier.com

Jo Duck
www.joduck.com

Vanessa Ellis
www.vanessaellis.co.uk

Fine Little Day
www.finelittleday.com

Mollie Flatley
www.norajane.etsy.com

Erin Freuchtel-Dearing
www.imaginationkidstoys.com

Funnelcloud Studio
www.funnelcloudstudio.com

Julie Garland
www.juliegarland.etsy.com

Helle Gavin
www.gavinsdukkehus.blogspot.com

Blanca González
www.cangaway.blogspot.com

Jenny Gordy
www.wikstenmade.com

Lauren Haupt Estes
www.laurenhauptjewelry.com

Eveline de Heij
www.bagonia.nl

Hurley Sashimi
www.hurleysashimi.com

Natalie Jost
www.nataliejost.com

Wendy Jung
www.wendyjung.co.uk

Just Noey
www.justnoey.com

Judy Kaufmann
www.kaufmannillustration.com

Stéphanie Kilgast
www.petitplat.fr

Kristen Beinke Photography
www.kristenbeinke.com

J. Blake Larson
blake.larson1@gmail.com

LAYERxlayer
www.layerxlayer.com

Eve Legris
www.evajuliet.com

Letterpress Delicacies
www.letterpressdelicacies.com

Lara Lewis
www.laralewis.net

Emīlija Lielā
www.karmatank.com

Little O by wolfbrother
www.littleobywolfbrother.etsy.com

Emily Lockhart
www.emilylockhart.ca

Becky McNeel
www.beckymcneel.com

MaaPstudio
www.maapstudio.com

Mae
www.lovemae.com.au

Katie Marcus
www.whatkatiedoes.net

Heather Moore
www.skinnylaminx.com

Brandy Murphy
www.of-the-fountain.com

Jenny Nguyen
www.jennyndesign.com

Izabela Nikiel
www.belastitches.etsy.com

Pawling Print Studio
www.pawlingprintstudio.com

Peg and Awl
www.pegandawlbuilt.com

Lucy Pope
www.lucypope.com

Pretty Swell
www.prettyswell.etsy.com

Megan Price
www.meganprice.com

Jennifer Putzier
www.isette.com

Helen Rawlinson
www.helenrawlinson.com

Rifle Paper Co.
www.riflepaperco.com

Erin Riley
www.fotographer.ca

Kristy Risser
www.californiacraft.etsy.com

Amity Roach
www.allthosethrees.etsy.com

Roee Raifeld
www.roeeraifeld.blogspot.com

Anastasia Shelyakina
www.laccentnou.etsy.com

Silly Buddy
www.silly-buddy.com

Simpli Jessi
www.simplijessi.etsy.com

Slide Sideways
www.slidesideways.etsy.com

Society Hill Designs
www.societyhilldesigns.com

A Sparkly Pony
www.sparklypony.com

Sweet Fine Day
www.sweetfineday.com

Huiyi Tan
www.huiyitan.com

Alan Tansey
www.alantansey.com

Tori Tedesco
www.littlebirdiedesign.etsy.com

Christine Tenenholtz
www.redhotpottery.etsy.com

Linda Thalmann
www.paperphine.com

These Are Things
www.thesearethings.com

Three 5 Eighty 5
www.threefiveeightyfive.etsy.com

Tooli's Jewelry
www.toolisjewelry.etsy.com

Tytie
www.tytie.com

Untamed Petals
www.untamedpetals.etsy.com

Craig VanDerSchaegen
www.craigvanders.com

Lisa Warninger
www.lisawarninger.com

Nora Whynot
www.norawhynot.com.au

Phil Wilkinson
Scotland, UK

Matthew Williams
www.matthewwilliamsphotographer.com

Robyn Wilson-Owen
www.robynlouisewilson.blogspot.com

Alarna Zinn
www.littlejanestreet.com.au

Crafters' Details

Arranged alphabetically according to surname if individual name and first word if company name

Heidi Adnum
www.heidiadnum.com
pages 4 and 5
page 19, image 2
page 50, image 2
page 53, image 3
page 137
pages 140 and 141
pages 168 and 169

Robyn Adnum
E: *robynadnum@gmail.com*
page 89

Amanda Jo Jewellery
www.amandajo.com.au
page 97

Jennifer Arndt
www.jenniferarndt.etsy.com
page 46, image 1

Bagman and Robin
www.bagmanandrobin.com
page 81

Bailey Doesn't Bark
www.baileydoesntbark.com
page 44, image 2
page 46, image3
page 181, all images

Meg Bartholomy
www.olliegraphic.com
page 119, image 3
page 171, image 1

Marie Bee
www.marie-bee.com
page 11, image 2

Bespoke Letterpress
www.bespokeletterpress.com.au
page 49, image 3
page 50, image 3

John Birdsong
www.johnbirdsong.etsy.com
page 45, image 4

California Craft
www.californiacraft.etsy.com
page 127, image 3

Celia Boaz
www.glitzglitter.etsy.com
page 13, image 2
page 93

Stacey Bradley
www.perlaanne.etsy.com
pages 116 and 117
pages 122 and 123
page 164, image 1

Lisa Bruemmer
www.treeandkimball.etsy.com
page 95, images 4 and 6

Bunnys
www.bunnys.etsy.com
pages 168–169, all images

Clair Catillaz
www.clamlab.com
page 109, image 3
page 115, all images

Michelle Chang
www.michellechang.com
page 99, all images

Chessell Ware
www.chessellpotterybarns.co.uk
page 55

Pei Li Chin
www.peiliminiatures.com
page 102, image 2

Rodica Cioplea
www.rodi-art.com
page 16, image 1

Timor Cohen
www.timo-handmade.com
page 38, image 2

Collective Approach
www.editbyedit.co.uk
page 43, image 4

Contrary Jewelry
www.contrary.etsy.com
page 94, images 2 and 3

Olga Courtnage
www.knittles.ca
page 85

Darlingtonia Moccasin Company
www.darlingtoniamoccasins.com
page 17, image 4
page 79, image 5

das linoleum
www.daslinoleum.etsy.com
page 121

Deliverance County
www.deliverancecounty.com
page 113

Helen Dickson
www.bustleandsew.blogspot.com
pages 66 and 67
page 167

Dimdi
www.dimdi.etsy.com
page 39

William Dohman
www.ohdier.com
page 47, image 4
page 139, all images

Fifi Flyaway
www.fififlyaway.etsy.com
page 59

Fine Little Day
www.finelittleday.com
page 34
page 38, image 1
page 133
page 135, image 6

Mollie Flatley
www.norajane.etsy.com
page 40, image 2

Erin Freuchtel-Dearing
www.imaginationkidstoys.com
page 107, all images

Funnelcloud Studio
www.funnelcloudstudio.com
page 40, image 1

Helle Gavin
www.gavinsdukkehus.blogspot.com
page 101

Gamanje Merchants
www.wildernesslodges.co.ke/keekorok_info.html
page 61, all images

Julie Garland
www.juliegarland.etsy.com
page 95, image 5

Bev Gill
T: +61 (0)2 6541 2441
page 15
page 53, image 3

Blanca González
www.cangaway.blogspot.com
page 100
page 102, images 1 and 3

Jenny Gordy
www.wikstenmade.com
page 91, all images
page 171, image 4

Gray Works Interpretive Furniture Design
www.grayworksdesign.etsy.com
page 41, image 6

Jessi Halliday
www.simplijessi.etsy.com
page 41, image 5

Lauren Haupt Estes
www.laurenhauptjewelry.com
page 44, image 3

Eveline de Heij
www.bagonia.nl
page 21, image 4

Hurley Sashimi
www.hurleysashimi.com
page 87, image 5
page 163

Samantha Holmes
www.samanthaholmes.com
page 86, image 2

Hopeless
www.hopeless.etsy.com
page 49, image 5

ila Handbags
www.ilahandbags.com
page 23, image 3
page 77, image 2

Jonny's Sister
www.jonnyssister.co.uk
page 14, image 1
page 19, image 3
page 27, image 2
page 87, image 4

Natalie Jost
www.nataliejost.com
page 27, image 3
page 32
page 48, image 2
page 52, image 2
page 177, image 2

Wendy Jung
www.wendyjung.co.uk
page 109, image 1

Just Noey
www.justnoey.com
page 40, image 3

Judy Kaufmann
www.kaufmannillustration.com
page 33
page 37, image 3
page 118
page 179

Stéphanie Kilgast
www.petitplat.fr
page 47, image 5

Gur Kimel
www.gurkimel.etsy.com
page 164, image 2

Kiss My Mutt
www.kissmymutt.etsy.com
page 42

Lamboro Crafts
Pembrokeshire, Wales, UK
page 105

LAYERxlayer
www.layerxlayer.com
page 19, image 4
page 79, image 3

Eve Legris
www.evajuliet.com
page 7
page 50, image 1
page 119, image 2

Letterpress Delicacies
www.letterpressdelicacies.com
page 25, image 2

Lara Lewis
www.laralewis.net
page 92

Emīlija Lielā
www.karmatank.com
pages 8 and 9
page 86, image 1

Little O by wolfbrother
www.littleobywolfbrother.etsy.com
page 41, image 4

MaaPstudio
www.maapstudio.com
page 94, image 1

Mae
www.lovemae.com.au
page 20, image 1
page 135, image 4

Manual Creative
www.editbyedit.co.uk
page 43, image 5

Katie Marcus
www.whatkatiedoes.net
page 28

Monique Martinez
www.ouma.etsy.com
page 11, image 3

Heather Moore
www.skinnylaminx.info
page 75, all images

Brandy Murphy
www.of-the-fountain.com
page 25, image 3

Jenny Nguyen
www.jennyndesign.com
page 76, image 1
page 79, image 4
page 83, all images

Izabela Nikiel
www.belastitches.etsy.com
page 171, image 3
page 174, image 2

Nitzan – Edit
www.editbyedit.co.uk
page 43, image 3

Overall Baby
www.overallbaby.com
page 69

Pete Oyler
www.peteoyler.com
page 10, image 1

Pawling Print Studio
www.pawlingprintstudio.com
page 43, image 2
page 78, image 1

Peg and Awl
www.pegandawlbuilt.com
page 20, image 2
page 124

Pigeon Toe Ceramics
www.pigeontoeceramics.com
page 18
page 21, image 3
page 51, image 4
page 109, image 2
page 110, image 1

pi'lo
www.pilosale.etsy.com
page 46, image 2
page 48, image 1
page 103, image 4

Pretty Swell
www.prettyswell.etsy.com
page 134, image 2

Megan Price
www.meganprice.com
page 37, image 2

Purl Alpaca Designs Ltd.
www.purlalpacadesigns.com
page 70, images 1 and 2

Jennifer Putzier
www.isette.com
page 24

Scott Rawlings
www.fullgive.etsy.com
page 77, image 3
page 78, image 2

Helen Rawlinson
www.helenrawlinson.com
page 71, image 4

Rifle Paper Co.
www.riflepaperco.com
page 36
page 44, image 1
page 131, all images
pages 172 and 173, all images

Amity Roach
www.allthosethrees.etsy.com
page 27, image 4

Rover
www.roverdog.blogspot.com
page 13, image 1

Kate Samphier
www.katesamphier.com
page 87, image 3

sealmaiden
www.sealmaiden.etsy.com
page 73

Shelbyville
www.shelbyville.com.au
page 129

Anastasia Shelyakina
www.laccentnou.etsy.com
page 17, image 3

Silly Buddy
www.silly-buddy.com
page 53, image 4
page 71, image 5

Slide Sideways
www.slidesideways.etsy.com
page 26

Margaret Smith
T: +61 (0)2 6562 8392
page 12

Society Hill Designs
www.societyhilldesigns.com
page 22

A Sparkly Pony
www.sparklypony.com
page 134, image 1

Sweet Fine Day
www.slidesideways.etsy.com
page 30
page 135, image 5

Tabaka Heritage
www.wildernesslodges.co.ke/keekorok_info.html
page 63

Huiyi Tan
www.huiyitan.com
page 17, image 5

Tori Tedesco
www.littlebirdiedesign.etsy.com
page 70, image 3

Christine Tenenholtz
www.redhotpottery.etsy.com
page 11, image 4
page 111, image 4

Linda Thalmann
www.paperphine.com
page 17, image 2

These Are Things
www.thesearethings.com
page 23, image 2

Three 5 Eighty 5
www.threefiveeightyfive.etsy.com
page 52, image 1

Tooli's Jewelry
www.toolisjewelry.etsy.com
page 57
page 171, image 2

Tytie
www.tytie.com
page 132
page 134, image 3

Untamed Petals
www.untamedpetals.etsy.com
page 49, image 4

Nora Whynot
www.norawhynot.com.au
page 126
page 127, image 4
page 174, image 1
page 175, image 3

Robyn Wilson-Owen
www.robynlouisewilson.blogspot.com
page 29

Alarna Zinn
www.littlejanestreet.com.au
page 110, image 2
page 111, image 3
page 125
page 176

Index

Acknowledgments

First of all, thank you for reading. I hope you found inspiration to take great photographs that bring you the success you deserve.

To all the contributors who I've had the pleasure of working with during this project, thank you for generously taking the time to send me your beautiful photographs. I feel privileged to work with a community of so many talented, creative, and driven people.

Big thanks to Isheeta Mustafi and RotoVision for approaching me with the opportunity to write this book and to Interweave and Search Press for publishing it. Thank you also to Lindy Dunlop and Jeannie Labno for their support and editorial guidance, and Emily Portnoi for the illustrations and design work.

Thanks also to the effervescent team at Etsy for providing me, and people like me, with a platform to promote the handmade lifestyle, allowing us to indulge in a career we love from the comfort of our own home or studio. In particular, I'd like to thank Amity Roach for the opportunity to become more involved.

Thank you to my fabulous friends, both near and far. Especially my darling Melanie, thank you for the daily doses of support, encouragement, and hilarity.

To my family and dearest Mum and Dad, thank you, there truly is no place like home.

And to my beautiful Will. Thank you for the unwavering support, constant encouragement, uber-calm, intelligent reasoning, and, of course, love. I couldn't have done this without you. I really am the luckiest.